Publisher: Military History Group, London

E-Mail: milhisgroup@gmail.com

Print: Lulu Press, Inc., Lulu Press, Inc. 62 NC 27560, USA. Massachusetts, US; Wisc__. France, France; Wielkopolska, Poland; Cambridgeshire, United __ _ Victoria, Australia.

Text © 2024 Peter Samsonov. Foreword © 2024 Markus Pöhlmann. Preface © 2024 Ralf Raths. All Rights reserved.

Cover design © by Julien Lepelletier.

Photographs & illustrations © as individually credited.

Any total or partial reproduction, copying, representation, adaptation, modification, or transfer of this book, its content or visuals, whether for commercial or non-commercial purposes, is forbidden without express, prior and written consent by the authors.

Quotations of the book with proper citation (authors, title, page number) are of course allowed.

978-1-915453-20-4

http://militaryhistorygroup.com

- Foreword by Markus Pöhlmann ... 4
- Preface by Ralf Raths ... 10
- Introduction ... 11
- Tiger Basics ... 12
  - Armor ... 13
  - Characteristics ... 14
  - The Tiger Timeline ... 16
- The Soviet View ... 19
  - Debut at Leningrad ... 19
  - Testing the Armor ... 25
  - Guns to Kill a Tiger ... 37
  - Testing the Tiger's Gun ... 48
  - The German Reaction ... 57
  - Tiger Tactics ... 61
  - How to Kill a Tiger Tank ... 65
  - Anti-Tiger Ammunition ... 72
  - Further Trials and Research ... 74
  - Conclusions ... 85
- The Anglo-American View ... 87
  - Debut in North Africa ... 87
  - Study of Tiger #131 ... 95
  - Penetration Trials in North Africa ... 105
  - Observation from the Tiger ... 114
  - Testing the Gun ... 119
  - Rematch in Italy ... 122
  - British Tiger Hunters ... 130
  - American Tiger Hunters ... 136
  - The Tiger's Last Bow ... 143
  - Penetration Trials at the End of the War ... 148

- Motion Studies 154
- Metallurgical Analysis 161
- Conclusions 166
- Myth or Legend? 168
- Appendix 1: Glossary 170
- Appendix 2: Preliminary Instructions on Combating Tigers 174
- Appendix 3: Memo to Soldiers, Sergeants, and Officers on Combat with German "Ferdinand" SPGs and "Tiger" Tanks 176
- Bibliography 181
  - Primary Sources 181
    - Russian Language Sources 181
    - English & German Language Sources 187
  - Secondary Sources 192
    - Websites 194

Foreword by Markus Pöhlmann[1]

"It Was a Real Tiger, the Real McCoy". Some Thoughts on *Panzer VI* and its Popular Imagination – Then and Now

When the Western Allies landed in Normandy in June 1944, the *Panzerkampfwagen VI (Ausf. E) Tiger* had already established a reputation among its enemies and as an established brand in German propaganda. After the war, a British tanker recalled his first visual encounter with the tank: "It was a real Tiger, the real McCoy. There was no doubt now, as we gazed up at its huge long gun [...] that here was the object of our nightmares."[2] The Tiger was a topic of conversation among the Allied soldiers and this reputation made its way into the veterans' memories and into popular culture. Today, when we think of tank warfare in the Second World War, we think of the Tiger or the T-34.

This special status deserves a closer look. One of the most eminent German experts, the director of the German Tank Museum, Ralf Raths, has tried to explain this appeal by the tank's good design.[3] Good design follows the universal law of the "Golden Ratio", which the Tiger fulfills with remarkable precision. The exterior impresses with its clear-cut shapes and empty surfaces. In addition, the tank's "deadliness of appearance" plays a role and also the fact that we can interpret the front view of the vehicle in a meaningful way.[4] The observer, Ralf Raths continues, interprets functional form in industrial design as "beautiful" – and this also applies to the tank design. Raths' ideas are as thought-provoking as they are incomplete – a fact that he himself acknowledges.

---

[1] Dr. Markus Pöhlmann is a military historian and a senior staff member of the German Armed Forces' Center for Military History and Social Sciences in Potsdam. His focus is German military history of the 19th to 21st century and intelligence history.

[2] Stephen Dyson of the 107th Regiment Royal Armoured Corps (The King's Own), quoted in John Buckley, *British Armour in the Normandy Campaign 1944*, Routledge, London and New York, 2014, p.188.

[3] Ralf Raths, *Der Bauhaus Panzer? Der Tiger I als Objekt des Industriedesigns* [The Bauhaus Tank? Tiger I as an Object of Industrial Design], https://www.youtube.com/watch?v=iE22h16Bxnc retrieved on 23rd January 2024.

[4] This cognitive effect, known as "pareidolia", allows us to recognize faces or bodies in certain objects.

The first question that arises is whether "beauty" can be a category for war machines at all. The term "sublimity", long-established in the history of technology, would probably be more appropriate. A tank is never "beautiful", but it can certainly have a sublime appearance. Whether this is actually the case with the Tiger with its bulky turret, however, is in the eye of the beholder.

The second question concerns the limited perspective: the visual appearance of the Tiger's exterior, i.e. the hull, turret, gun and tracks, is undoubtedly only one part of the vehicle among many when it comes to the significance of a weapon system in popular culture. So let's take the argument of good design as a bold first serve and take up the suggestion. What other categories can help explain the impact of the Tiger?

First of all, there is the rather banal fact that the Tiger was the first German tank with a suggestive name.[5] It thus established a zoological tradition in the German *Panzerwaffe* that still exists today. *Panzerkampfwagen VI (Ausf. E)* or *Sd.KfZ 181* would have been showstoppers during any campfire yarn of the soldiers. "Tiger" was the name of the beast.

Furthermore, the timing when the Tiger arrived on the battlefield was also decisive for its reputation. The year 1942 was an existential crisis and a turning point in the history of the German *Panzerwaffe*. The Tiger stands for this crisis.[6] At the end of 1941, the period of rapid operations against inferior or isolated opponents had come to an end. In the Soviet Union, the *Wehrmacht* had entered a deadly realm of attrition. For the *Panzerwaffe*, 1942 was first and foremost a crisis of doctrine. The stiffening Soviet resistance forced a hectic expansion in tank destroyers and assault guns. These systems were more closely tied to the infantry and they drew resources from tank procurement. Under these conditions, deep, independent tank operations were increasingly difficult to think about and plan. Above all, 1942 was also a crisis of hardware. When the German experts studied the captured T-34s in fall 1941, they realized that time was running out for their tried and tested medium Panzer III and IV types. The

---

[5] Porsche's earlier "Leopard" (VK 30.01 (P)) from 1939 remained a prototype that was never to see the light of day.

[6] For this crisis, see Markus Pöhlmann, *Der Panzer und die Mechanisierung des Krieges. Eine deutsche Geschichte 1890 bis 1945*, F. Schöningh, Paderborn, 2016, pp.341-373.

development for the new types, the medium Panzer V (Panther) and the heavy Panzer VI (Tiger) now became an acute need.

1942 was also a veritable crisis for German armaments. The failure of Operation *Barbarossa* had enforced Hitler's personal commitment to the issue of tanks. This was not without reason, as the pre-war system of military command economy had obviously suffered shipwreck in matters of development and industrial coordination. Now new, more powerful types of tanks were needed in large numbers. Enter the Tiger!

The rushed procurement and production process between April and October 1942 brought German tank procurement to its limit, which also explains the technical teething troubles of this tank. Nevertheless, by the end of the year, a next-generation tank was rolling. Even though the Tiger was immediately deployed in North Africa, the *Wehrmacht's* expectations were primarily focused on the use of the new weapon system on the Eastern Front. In 1943, the Tiger – together with the Panther – was to become a game changer.[7] The multiple crises in strategy, doctrine, hardware, and armament therefore guaranteed the Tiger increased attention from tank experts, but also from ordinary *Wehrmacht* soldiers, from 1942 onwards.

There was another aspect to this: With the end of the so-called *Blitzkrieg* period, *Wehrmacht* propaganda was also forced to develop new strategies. The generational change in tank technology described above came in very handy, as it promised impressive images of fearsome war machines. However, the renewal of the German propaganda strategy was not only about new images, but also about new narratives. Stories now had to be developed that were more about individual strength of will, successful resistance against superior forces and technical prowess in a war of attrition. The prominent *Panzer* generals of 1939-41, such as Heinz Guderian or Erwin Rommel, were no longer in the center of attention. Instead, the propaganda increasingly focused on junior officers and crew members – "average" dudes with stubbly beards and high killing scores. These new *Panzer* aces could only be promoted in conjunction with their vehicle,

---

[7] For this expectation, see Roman Töppel, *Kursk 1943: The Greatest Battle of the Second World War*, Helion, Solihull, 2018.

and the vehicle of choice from 1942 onwards was the Tiger. Hardly anyone today would associate Otto Carius with the *Panzer 38 (t)*, in which he was still fighting in 1941. Only sophisticated tank nerds will think of a *Panzer IV* when they hear the name Kurt Knispel. Nor can one imagine Michael Wittmann in the *Sturmgeschütz III* that he was still commanding in 1941. The whole popular concept of the *Panzer* aces was and is still very closely linked to one particular type of tank, and that is the Tiger.

However, the Tiger is not simply a product of the *Wehrmacht's* effective propaganda. Under particular conditions, it was also quite simply a deadly weapon system that could dominate the battlefield with an 8.8 cm KWK 36 cannon, a frontal armor up to 100 mm, a well-trained crew and a tactical commander who was aware of its strengths and weaknesses. However, low mobility, technical vulnerability and insufficient production numbers always limited this 'Tiger scenario'. It always remained the exception between 1942 and 1945, it was never the norm. But these real deficits do not seem to have diminished the appeal of this tank in popular imagination.

The effective fighting power of the Panzer VI was also recognized by its opponents. And their stories about the Tiger also played a significant role in military historiography and the popular imagination. A genuine recognition for the Tiger's technical and tactical advantages played a role in this. But the enemy soldier's own victory was also most effective when it was achieved against such a powerful opponent. In the heat of battle, you might have seen a Tiger where there had perhaps 'only' been a *Panzer IV*. This brings us to Peter Samsonov's book.

The process of identifying a new weapon on the opponent's side, understanding it and developing one's own techniques, tactics and procedures was and it still is determined by a multitude of sources and by extreme time pressure. The Allies' reaction to the appearance of the Tiger is an excellent case study in this respect. This process of military learning begins with the imagination phase. Some innovations are 'in the air'. Intelligence services receive first indications, they provide individual photos. The weapon might have already appeared on other fronts, but not yet on one's own. This first phase of imagination is characterized by assumptions, rumors, and false reports.

The second phase is the encounter. Aerial photos and combat reports are now available. If we take the example of the Tiger, the first parameters such as its shape and the range of its primary weapon have now been clarified. How long this phase lasts depends heavily on the weapon system. In the case of tanks, which by definition came close to the enemy and which were sometimes difficult to recover from a contested battlefield, this phase remained relatively short. Sooner or later, a damaged enemy tank could be inspected on site or even recovered.

This marked the beginning of the third phase, the evaluation. The moment the slain beast had been dragged into the cave, the military knowledge apparatus began to run. The captured tank was photographed, sketched, weighed, measured, shot at and – as far as possible – driven on the training ground. The individual components were dismantled and reassembled. This was the time of the motor engineers, the experts in ballistics, metallurgy and industrial manufacturing. But it was also the time for interrogators and translators, because captured tank crews and captured documents could provide important information. In this phase, the aim was to combine scientific findings and tactical experience into an initial, meaningful picture.

The fourth phase was the implementation of these findings in procedures and the adaptation of the hardware. Of course, this phase could start much earlier here and there. The troops were informed about the appearance of the Tiger and first indications of possible weak points of the vehicle were given in lectures and provisional pamphlets. The troops did not wait for instructions from above, but began to think independently about adapting their tactics. Military learning in modern armed forces never only works top-down. Many insights grow bottom-up, and also through a horizontal exchange of information. Peter Samsonov impressively analyzes how all levels of the military hierarchy thought about and decided on the adaptation of their own armored fighting vehicles, their anti-tank weaponry and their ammunition. These adaptation processes were limited only by the urgency of the problem and the availability of resources. The special thing about technical evaluation in the Second World War was that new weapon systems appeared on different fronts almost simultaneously and could lead to different conclusions there. An encounter with a single Tiger in the rugged Tunisian hills could leave a completely different impression of the Tiger's potential than an encounter with a complete Tiger company supported by assault guns and tank artillery in open terrain somewhere in the Ukraine. These experiences also had to be synchronized across the different theaters of war. This exchange of information between the Red Army experts and the Western Allies was one of the most interesting aspects of military learning. It worked well in the case of the Tiger (but not in the case of the Panther).[8]

The ability of armed forces and the societies behind them to understand technological change in modern war and to push it to the advantage of their own side contributes just as much to victory or defeat as the martial qualities of their soldiers. The subject of this book is therefore only at first glance one of nuts and bolts. After a careful reading, the question arises as to how much today's armed forces have this ability and how they could bring it to bear on the very different battlefield of the 21st Century.

---

[8] See Bradley F. Smith, *Sharing Secrets with Stalin. How the Allies Traded Intelligence, 1941-1945*, University Press of Kansas, Lawrence KS, 1996, pp.191-193.

Preface by Ralf Raths[9]

Military history books come in a wide variety of flavors today. One can for example dive into the depths of theory in the books of Jeremy Black, written in a distinctly academical style. One can enjoy the gripping panoramas of Robert Citino and get a feeling for the "flesh" of military history. One can enjoy the dry sarcasm of Dennis Showalter's works. Readers can try to poke holes into classical narratives or try to wrap their heads around flashy hypotheses in countless new books.

Often overlooked by the general audience though are the "grunts" of the military history book market: Books that relentlessly bore into a narrowly defined corpus of sources and mine them for information. This kind of book practically never reaches great sales numbers due to their by nature often rather tedious style, but they are indispensable for the progress of military history: The information extracted and made available in such books are the foundation on which broad the sweeping panoramas and/or daring theories in bestsellers can be built upon.

Peter Samsonov's "Achtung Tiger!" is exactly such a meritorious "grunt" book. The scope of sources is deliberately narrow, but their contents are presented cohesively and usably. What has been scattered all over the world, hidden in archives, is now neatly available in one concise book – and therefore discussions regarding the topic "What could penetrate a Tiger's armor?" can be guided by facts instead of feelings from now on.

And don't be mistaken: Though it might not be what publishers call a 'pageturner', it is by no means boring. Samsonsov has to present an abundance of data on the results of penetration tests to fulfill the book's purpose, but time and time again he adds context that is highly interesting. This includes for example details as to why some tests were conducted in the way they were. But more importantly, it also includes contemporary conclusions, impressions and opinions that often have long since been falsified by historical research – but are absolutely logical and plausible in their historical context.

---

[9] Ralf Raths is a military historian and director of the German Tank Museum at Munster.

Introduction

The Tiger tank earned a special reputation among tanks of the Second World War. Even though only 1347 vehicles of this type were built between 1942 and 1944[10], a disproportionate amount of media focuses on this tank. Popular history outlets such as the History Channel paint the tank as "impervious to attack" and claim that "the mere whisper of its name would inspire panic and terror".[11] While the Tiger tank indeed was a powerful weapon in the German arsenal, Allied officers and weapons designers responded to it in a calm and measured manner. Samples of the Tiger tank were obtained and studied, existing weapons tested, and new ones put into production where old ones failed. If anything, the impression formed by the author over the course of a decade of reading, translating, and analyzing primary documents is that other German vehicles (particularly the Panther and the Ferdinand) were considered to be more serious and immediate threats, requiring more radical solutions. This book will examine how engineers, tankers, anti-tank gunners, and even infantrymen studied, fought, and defeated the Tiger tank.

---

[10] H. Doyle and T. Jentz, *Tiger I Heavy Tank 1942-1945*, Osprey Publishing, Oxford, 1993, pp.11-13

[11] Military Channel, *Top Ten Tanks #3: Tiger*,
https://www.youtube.com/watch?v=qoyW83fdJi4, retrieved on February 16th, 2024

Tiger Basics

This book contains many technical details of the Tiger tank as recorded by Soviet, American, and British specialists. These values could be distorted by human error in measurement and incorrect intelligence. Additionally, characteristics of any individual Tiger could vary from nominal specifications and measurements obtained from one Tiger tank would not necessarily be true for the next. The official characteristics of the Tiger tank are provided here for the reader's reference, so that they can judge for themselves what the Allies got right and wrong about the Tiger.

Tiger 131, Bovington Tank Museum. This was the first Tiger tank captured intact by British forces. Study of this vehicle revealed a lot about the new German tank and German tank industry in general. *(Peter Samsonov)*

Armor

Thicknesses of the Tiger's armor plates. These are nominal figures and thicknesses for individual vehicles could differ.[12] Note that the basic thickness of the gun mantlet is nominally 90 mm with local reinforcement around the gun (200 mm) and gun sight (150 mm) openings. British analysis indicated that this kind of composite armor is unlikely to offer protection exceeding that of an ordinary 100 mm thick plate.[13]

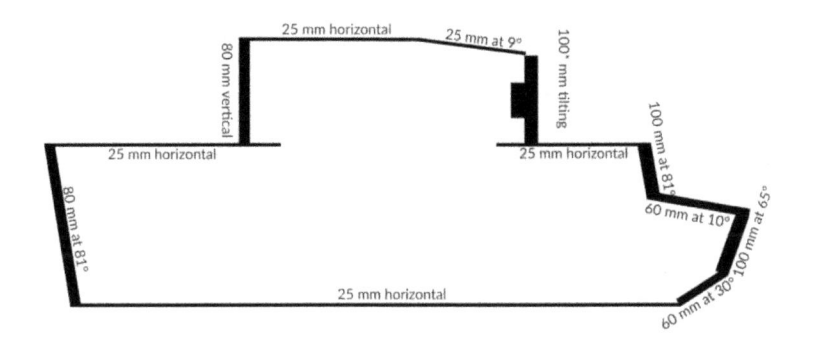

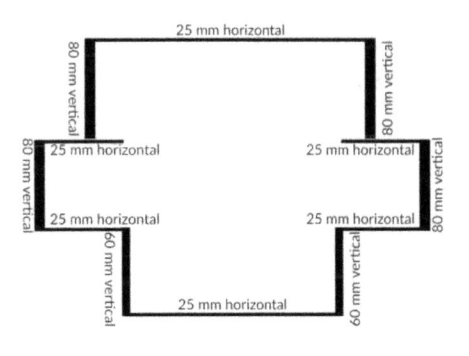

---

[12] H. Doyle and T. Jentz, *Germany's Tiger Tanks D.W. to Tiger I: Design, Production & Modifications*, Schiffer Publishing, Ltd, 2000, p.34

[13] Canadian Military Headquarters, London (CMHQ), Files Block No. 55 - 5773, Image 1394

Characteristics

Official characteristics from *Wa Prüf 6* as of November 1st, 1943[14] and Henschel as of February 9th, 1944.[15]

	Wa Prüf 6	Henschel
Combat weight	54,000 kg	57,000 kg
Top speed	45 kph	45.4 kph
Top sustainable speed		
Good roads	30 kph	40 kph
Average terrain	20-25 kph	20-25 kph
Dimensions		
Length with gun forward	8451 mm	8450 mm
Length without gun overhang	6280 mm	6316 mm
Width with battle tracks	3560 mm	3547 mm
Width with transport tracks	3230 mm	3142 mm
Full height	3000 mm	3000 mm[16] 2885 mm[17]
Ground pressure	1.03 kg/cm²	1.05 kg/cm²

---

[14] H. Doyle and T. Jentz, *Germany's Tiger Tanks D.W. to Tiger I: Design, Production & Modifications*, Schiffer Publishing, Ltd, 2000, p.177

[15] H. Doyle and T. Jentz, *Germany's Tiger Tanks D.W. to Tiger I: Design, Production & Modifications*, Schiffer Publishing, Ltd, 2000, p.179

[16] With early turret

[17] With late turret equipped with a lower profile cupola

Armament		
Main gun	8.8 cm KwK 36	8.8 cm KwK 36
Main gun ammunition	92	92
Machine guns	2	2
Machine gun ammunition	4500	4800
Submachine guns	1	1
Submachine gun ammunition	192	192

The Tiger Timeline

November 1938	Commander-in-Chief of the German Army *Generaloberst* Walther von Brauchitsch orders the creation of assault tanks with 80 mm thick frontal armor.[18]
May 1941	Hitler increases the requirements for new heavy tanks. They must now have an 88 mm gun.[19]
Unknown	A decision is made to mass produce the new tank. Plans are made for a pilot series of 100 units.[20]
September 1941	Owing to the requirement for an 88 mm gun, Henschel is forced to use the same turret as the Porsche heavy tank, widening the chassis and reaching a weight of 45 tons. The new Henschel and Porsche projects are designated VK 45.01 (fully tracked, 45 ton weight class, 1st type).[21]
April 1942	Henschel's VK 45.01 (H) and Porsche's VK 45.01 (P) tanks are presented to Hitler on his birthday.[22] An additional 200 VK 45.01 (H) tanks are ordered.[23]
August 1942	An additional 124 VK 45.01 (H) tanks are ordered.[24] The first production Tiger tanks are delivered to the army.[25]

---

[18] Y. Pasholok, *V poluschage ot Tigra*, https://warspot.ru/10152-v-polushage-ot-tigra, retrieved on February 16th, 2024

[19] Y. Pasholok, *Tigr Porsche: zhertva gryaznoy konkurentsii*, https://warspot.ru/10435-tigr-porshe-zhertva-gryaznoy-konkurentsii, retrieved on February 16th, 2024

[20] H. Doyle and T. Jentz, *Germany's Tiger Tanks D.W. to Tiger I: Design, Production & Modifications*, Schiffer Publishing, Ltd, 2000, p.67

[21] H. Doyle and T. Jentz, *Germany's Tiger Tanks D.W. to Tiger I: Design, Production & Modifications*, Schiffer Publishing, Ltd, 2000, p.31

[22] Y. Pasholok, *Tigr Porsche: zhertva gryaznoy konkurentsii*, https://warspot.ru/10435-tigr-porshe-zhertva-gryaznoy-konkurentsii, retrieved on February 16th, 2024

[23] H. Doyle and T. Jentz, *Germany's Tiger Tanks D.W. to Tiger I: Design, Production & Modifications*, Schiffer Publishing, Ltd, 2000, p.67

[24] H. Doyle and T. Jentz, *Germany's Tiger Tanks D.W. to Tiger I: Design, Production & Modifications*, Schiffer Publishing, Ltd, 2000, p.28

[25] H. Doyle and T. Jentz, *Germany's Tiger Tanks D.W. to Tiger I: Design, Production & Modifications*, Schiffer Publishing, Ltd, 2000, p.68

September 1942	Tiger tanks go into battle for the first time on the Leningrad Front.[26]
November 1942	Prototypes of the tanks (now called Pz.Kpfw.VI P and Pz.Kpfw.VI H) go through comparative trials at Bad Berka. The Pz.Kpfw.VI H is declared the winner. Pz.Kpfw.VI P tanks that have already been completed are to be converted into tank destroyers.[27] 250 Pz.Kpfw.VI H tanks are ordered. Tiger production begins at full throttle.[28]
December 1942	Tiger tanks go into battle in Tunisia.[29]
January 1943	The first intact Tiger tanks are captured by the Soviets at Leningrad.[30] British troops get an opportunity to examine demolished Tiger tanks in Tunisia.[31]
April 1943	The Soviets hold penetration and gunnery trials of captured Tiger tanks.[32]
May 1943	The first intact Tiger tank, Tiger #131, is recovered by the British.[33]
July 1943	Tiger tanks are first used en masse at the Battle of Kursk. Notes on the operation of Tiger units are made by Soviet intelligence.[34]

---

[26] W. Schneider, *Tigers in Combat I*, Stackpole Books, Mechanicsburg, 2004 p.73

[27] H. Doyle and T. Jentz, *Germany's Tiger Tanks D.W. to Tiger I: Design, Production & Modifications*, Schiffer Publishing, Ltd, 2000, p.28

[28] H. Doyle and T. Jentz, *Germany's Tiger Tanks D.W. to Tiger I: Design, Production & Modifications*, Schiffer Publishing, Ltd, 2000, p.68

[29] W. Schneider, *Tigers in Combat I*, Stackpole Books, Mechanicsburg, 2004 p.42-43

[30] W. Schneider, *Tigers in Combat I*, Stackpole Books, Mechanicsburg, 2004 p.75

[31] W. Schneider, *Tigers in Combat I*, Stackpole Books, Mechanicsburg, 2004 p.43

[32] TsAMO RF F.38 Op.11377 D.12 L.1

[33] D. Oscroft, *The Myth of Tiger 131*, https://tankmuseum.org/article/the_myth_of_tiger_131, retrieved on November 6th, 2023

[34] TsAMO RF F.3384 Op1. D.13 L.18

June 1944	The Western Allies land in Normandy. The British first encounter large formations of Tiger tanks.[35]
August 1944	Tiger production ends with 1346 production tanks completed.[36]

---

[35] T. Schwallie, *Interview with Steven Zaloga*, https://tankandafvnews.com/2015/01/27/zaloga_interview/, retrieved on February 16th, 2024

[36] H. Doyle and T. Jentz, *Germany's Tiger Tanks D.W. to Tiger I: Design, Production & Modifications*, Schiffer Publishing, Ltd, 2000, p.68

The Soviet View

Debut at Leningrad

The city of Leningrad was a thorn in the side of Army Group North. German troops had to split their efforts between putting pressure on the city's garrison and resisting constant attempts made by the Red Army to relieve the besieged city or at least punch through the blockade to set up a more secure supply route. The swamps and forests around Leningrad favored the defender, and while this helped the Germans maintain the blockade it also limited their options when it came to counterattacks. Hitler insisted that Germany's newest tank be sent here and had great hopes for its performance.[37]

Four Tiger tanks were delivered to the *schwere Panzer-Abteilung* 502 (502nd Heavy Tank Battalion) in August of 1942. Despite the name, not every tank in the new formation was heavy. Early Tiger units contained 2 Tigers and 2 Pz.Kpfw.III tanks per platoon. With an authorized strength of four platoons per company plus a Tiger for the commander, the number of tanks gathered for the Tiger's debut was sufficient for less than half a company.[38] This would have to be enough. By the beginning of September, the first Tiger tanks detrained at Mga. Operation of these tanks was difficult and 3 out of 4 Tigers suffered transmission failure on the march to their defensive positions. The tanks returned to fighting shape within a few weeks and received their first combat orders on September 21st, 1942. The Tigers were to support the 170th Infantry Division and deliver an attack against the Soviet 2nd Shock Army at Tortolovo. This attack was a disaster for the Tigers. One tank was hit and even though the shell didn't penetrate the armor, this was enough to cause an engine malfunction. Three more Tigers bogged down in the swamp. Three of the disabled tanks were recovered, but the third remained in no man's land. German High Command strictly prohibited demolishing this tank.[39]

---

[37] H. Boog and others, *Das Deutsche Reich und der Zweite Weltkrieg 6: Der Globale Krieg.* Bd. 6, Deutsche Verlags-Anstalt, Stuttgart, Germany, 1990 (Das Deutsche Reich und der Zweite Weltkrieg 6), p.904

[38] W. Schneider, *Tigers in Combat I*, Stackpole Books, Mechanicsburg, 2004 p.4

[39] W. Schneider, *Tigers in Combat I*, Stackpole Books, Mechanicsburg, 2004 p.73

Fortunately for the Germans, the Soviet side took no notice of a new tank. No attempt was made to evacuate the Tiger or even send scouts to examine it.[40] Permission was finally given to demolish the tank on November 25th, 1942.[41]

It would not be too long before the Tigers saw battle once again. The Red Army was preparing for another offensive in the Leningrad sector. This offensive codenamed *Iskra* (Spark) involved an attack by elements of the Leningrad Front from the west and Volkhov Front from the east to create a land link to the besieged city along the coast of Lake Ladoga north of Mga. The offensive began on January 12th, 1943.[42] The 1st company of *schwere Panzer-Abteilung* 502 with 4 Tigers and 8 Pz.Kpfw.III tanks was sent north of the town of 1-y Gorodok to fight off Red Army troops crossing the Neva.[43] The Tigers could not achieve decisive success here either and soon began to go out of action once more. One Tiger with chassis number 250003 got stuck in a bog and demolished on January 17th, 1942. A Tiger tank with chassis number 250006 took hits to the front and even though the armor was not penetrated this was enough to take out the transmission. This tank was also demolished.[44] Soviet records indicate that this demolition was incomplete and one of these tanks was later used as a source of spare parts for Tigers undergoing trials.[45]

---

[40] A. Ulanov, D. Shein, *Perviye Tridtsatchetverki*, Tactical Press, Moscow, 2014 p.35
[41] W. Schneider, *Tigers in Combat I*, Stackpole Books, Mechanicsburg, 2004 p.74
[42] Y. Pasholok, *Tyazheliy Trofey*, https://warspot.ru/9797-tyazhyolyy-trofey, retrieved on October 26th, 2023
[43] W. Schneider, *Tigers in Combat I*, Stackpole Books, Mechanicsburg, 2004 p.74
[44] Y. Pasholok, *Tyazheliye trofei iz mesta proryva blokady Leningrada*, https://dzen.ru/a/Y7mBJbPX2DsnnkXi, retrieved on October 26th, 2023
[45] Y. Pasholok, *Tyazheliy Trofey*, https://warspot.ru/9797-tyazhyolyy-trofey, retrieved on October 26th, 2023

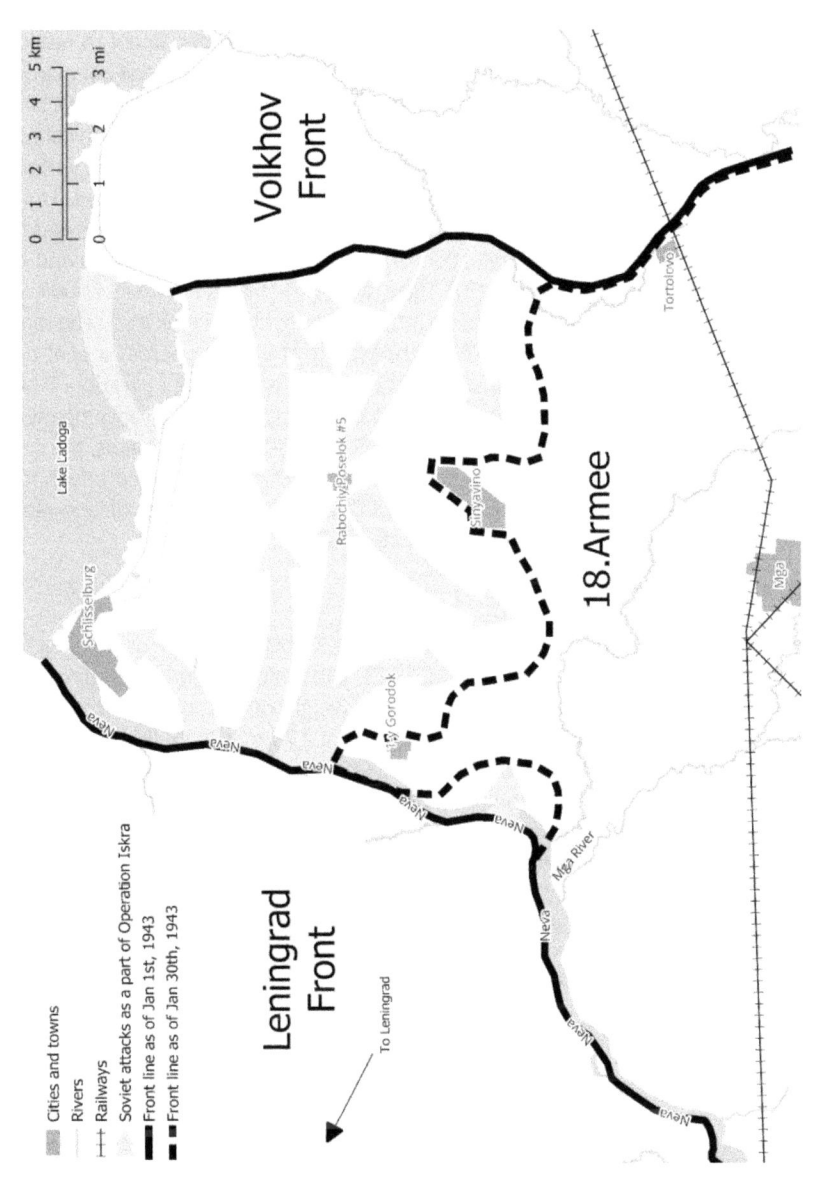

Map of the vicinity of Sinyavino, where Tiger tanks of *schwere Panzer-Abteilung* 502 fought their first battles. Even the use of the newest German heavy tank could not prevent the blockade of Leningrad from being breached. *(Peter Samsonov)*

As German defenses crumbled, the two Red Army Fronts aimed to meet at Rabochiy Poselok (Workers' Village) #5 north of Sinyavino. The 1st company of the *schwere Panzer-Abteilung* 502 was sent there to prevent the link and avoid encirclement, but the remaining Tiger tanks were lost in an almost comical way. A Tiger tank with chassis number 250004 and turret number 121 suffered engine failure and had to be abandoned as Soviet forces drew close. Unlike 250003 and 250006 that could be demolished before capture, this tank was left in a hurry with a complete collection of documents including manuals and the vehicle's maintenance logbook.[46] A Tiger tank with chassis number 250009 and turret number 100 was also captured intact at Rabochiy Poselok #5.[47] The tank's driver decided to take a shortcut on the way to the village across a peat bog. The tank fell into a pit left dug as a part of a peat harvesting operation. It was impossible for the crew to recover the tank on their own. With all accompanying Pz.Kpfw.III tanks destroyed and Rabochiy Poselok #5 in Soviet hands, the crew had no option but to withdraw, leaving Tiger #100 for the Soviets to find.[48] Within only a few days, the Red Army had captured four samples of Germany's newest tank, two of them in near-perfect condition.

This discovery was recorded in the reconnaissance summary of the Volkhov Front for January 15th-January 30th, 1943. The tank's weight was estimated at 75-80 tons (some 20 tons more than the real weight of 56 tons). The front armor was overestimated to be 110 mm thick with a 190 mm thick driver's visor (in reality, 100 mm thick). The side armor was underestimated at 75 mm for the hull and 65 mm for the turret. The rear and roof were measured fairly closely at 80 and 30 mm respectively (in reality, 82 and 25 mm). The tank was said to have one 88 mm main gun with 86 rounds of ammunition and two 7.60 mm machine guns (in reality, 7.92 mm). The tank had a Maybach engine that could run at up to 4000 RPM and a transmission with an 8-speed gearbox in the front. Even though the intelligence summary contains mistakes as listed above, this is undoubtedly a Tiger tank.[49] However, at this time the tank was known after a

---

[46] Y. Pasholok, *Tyazheliye trofei iz mesta proryva blokady Leningrada*, https://dzen.ru/a/Y7mBJbPX2DsnnkXi, retrieved on October 26th, 2023

[47] W. Schneider, *Tigers in Combat I*, Stackpole Books, Mechanicsburg, 2004 p.75

[48] Y. Pasholok, *Tyazheliye trofei iz mesta proryva blokady Leningrada*, https://dzen.ru/a/Y7mBJbPX2DsnnkXi, retrieved on October 26th, 2023

[49] TsAMO RF F.38 Op.11355 D.1712, L.31 *Vypiska iz itogovoy razvedsvodki #2 UBT i MV Volkhovskogo Fronta za period s 15.1 po 31.1.43*

different animal. Soviet troops called it "Elephant"[50] after a white elephant painted on the armor, the insignia of the *schwere Panzer-Abteilung* 502. The tanks were also referred to as "Henschel type captured tank" and "T-VI" in correspondence.[51] The index T-VI or T-6 persisted even after the name "Tiger" came into common use.[52] It is likely that the index was based on a captured manual, as the Red Army would have had no knowledge of the Pz.Kpfw.V (Panther) at this time.

Tiger #121 was sent to the NIBT Proving Grounds at Kubinka. Tiger #100 followed after it was repaired using components taken from the partially demolished Tiger. Tiger #121 was stripped of its components and prepared for penetration trials, while Tiger #100 would be used for mobility and gunnery trials.[53]

After trials, both Tiger #100 and the shot-up husk of Tiger #121 were displayed at the exhibition of captured enemy materiel at Gorky Park in Moscow. Neither tank survives to this day. The Tiger with turret number 100 displayed at Patriot Park at the time of writing is a late production model.

---

[50] P. Samsonov, *Tiger or Elephant?*, https://www.tankarchives.ca/2019/10/tiger-or-elephant.html, retrieved on October 26th, 2023

[51] Y. Pasholok, *Tyazheliy Trofey*, https://warspot.ru/9797-tyazhyolyy-trofey, retrieved on October 26th, 2023

[52] TsAMO RF F.38 Op.11355 D.2890 L.1 *Rezultaty zamerov usiliy na rychayakh upravleniya inostrannykh i otechestvennykh tankov*

[53] Y. Pasholok, *Tyazheliy Trofey*, https://warspot.ru/9797-tyazhyolyy-trofey, retrieved on October 26th, 2023

Tiger tank at the Patriot Park museum. Despite the same tactical number as one of the early Tigers, this is a much later model as indicated by the late style commander's cupola and leftover Zimmerit coating. *(Pavel Borovikov)*

Testing the Armor

The scope of the penetration trials held against Tiger #121 was quite large. 13 cannons, both foreign and domestic, were prepared for testing against the Tiger's armor. 10 more weapons were prepared, including 5 experimental anti-tank rifles, mines, grenades, and aircraft autocannons.[54] Trials lasted from April 25th to April 30th, 1943.[55] Unless otherwise stated, all shots were fired at 90 degrees to the armor plate targeted.

T-70 tank carrying a 45 mm model 1938 20-K gun, Museum of National Military History, Padikovo. Against a tank six times its weight, the T-70 was only effective at very close range. *(Pavel Borovikov)*

The first weapon used in the trial was a 45 mm model 1938 20-K gun installed on a T-70 tank. No attempt was made at firing regular armor piercing shells and trials were only carried out with subcaliber armor piercing shot with a muzzle velocity of 985 m/s (compared to 750 m/s for ordinary armor piercing shells).

---

[54] TsAMO RF F.38 Op.11377 D.12 L.1b
[55] TsAMO RF F.38 Op.11377 D.12 L.1

One hit on the side (82 mm thick) from 200 meters penetrated. The tungsten carbide core made a 20 mm hole as expected. A second shot at this range did not penetrate, leaving a 40 mm deep 20 mm wide hole. One shot was fired from 350 meters and one from 500. Neither penetrated. A shot fired at the lower side (62 mm) penetrated completely.[56] Further details on the use and development of special armor piercing ammunition to deal with Tiger tanks can be found in the chapter titled Anti-Tiger Ammunition.

45 mm model 1942 M-42 anti-tank gun, Museum of National Military History, Padikovo. This was a more powerful weapon with a longer barrel than the earlier 45 mm gun, but its effectiveness against the Tiger was still limited. *(Pavel Borovikov)*

The next weapon to be tested was the more powerful 45 mm model 1942 anti-tank gun. One attempt was made to penetrate the side of the tank with a BR-240 armor piercing shell with a muzzle velocity of 870 m/s. The shell failed to penetrate at a range of 100 meters, leaving a 30 mm deep dent. Further trials took place using the BR-240P subcaliber armor piercing shot with a muzzle velocity of 1070 m/s. In the same conditions, the shot penetrated the side of the hull, leaving behind a hole larger than the diameter of the tungsten carbide core: 22 mm on entry and 30 mm on exit.[57]

---

[56] TsAMO RF F.38 Op.11377 D.12 L.8-9
[57] TsAMO RF F.38 Op.11377 D.12 L.11

Four shots were fired from 350 meters. The results were still promising. Two penetrated the side of the turret (82 mm), leaving behind 20 mm holes. One made a 30 mm hole in the hull and created a crack in the armor, another shot to the hull broke off a 50x50 mm piece of armor. Two more shots from 500 meters failed to penetrate the upper side of the hull (82 mm) but one penetrated the lower side (62 mm).[58]

57 mm ZIS-2 anti-tank gun, Musée des Blindés, Saumur. The ZIS-2 was a light but powerful anti-tank weapon and had a good effect against the Tiger's armor. *(Peter Samsonov)*

The next weapon to be used was the 57 mm ZIS-2 anti-tank gun. One shot was fired at the side of the Tiger from 800 meters. The damage was much greater than the 45 mm gun caused; a 190x210 mm piece of armor broke off on the inside and a crack formed in the weld seam between the side and rear plate. The opening made by the hit was 110 mm in diameter at its narrowest point.

---

[58] TsAMO RF F.38 Op.11377 D.12 L.11-12

Another shot to the side from 1000 meters made a hole with a 110 mm wide entrance and 140 mm wide exit. A 140x110 mm piece of armor was dislodged. A second shot at this range did not penetrate. Still firing from 1000 meters, a third shot hit the commander's cupola and penetrated it leaving an 85x75 mm hole as well as tearing it off the turret. Three more shots were fired into the side of the turret from 1450 meters. Two led to a cracked bump forming on the inner side of the plate, but none resulted in a penetration.[59]

The front of the tank proved to be a tougher target. Three shots were fired from 500 meters, two at the upper front and one at the lower. The first ricocheted and hit the driver's visor. The second hit the machine gun ball and burst the weld seam holding the vertical and sloped plates together, but did not penetrate the armor. The third hit the lower front plate, also sending cracks through the weld seams that held it in place but not penetrating the main armor.[60]

The fourth gun to be tested against the Tiger tank was a foreign one. The "57 mm English anti-tank gun" or 6-pounder Mk.II fired armor piercing Mk.IIIT shot at a velocity of 822 m/s. Performance was similar to the Soviet 57 mm gun. At a range of 800 meters, it penetrated the side of the Tiger's turret, leaving an 82x75 mm hole. Two more shots to the side of the turret from 1000 meters at 30 degrees from normal and at normal failed to penetrate, leaving only bumps on the inside. A shot at the side of the hull from 1000 meters led to a penetration, leaving a hole 70 mm wide on entrance and 115 mm wide on exit. The gun was not fired against the front of the Tiger.[61]

Trials of a 6-pounder gun installed in a Churchill tank were also carried out. The gun fired the same ammunition. Only two shots were fired at a range of 625 meters. One hit the side of the tank and penetrated, leaving a 58 mm hole. The other hit the lower edge of the plate. This hit was not counted.[62]

---

[59] TsAMO RF F.38 Op.11377 D.12 L.14
[60] TsAMO RF F.38 Op.11377 D.12 L.14-17
[61] TsAMO RF F.38 Op.11377 D.12 L.18-20
[62] TsAMO RF F.38 Op.11377 D.12 L.21

Medium Tank M4A2, Victory Park, Moscow. The Sherman's 75 mm M3 gun was only effective against the Tiger's side armor at relatively close range. *(Pavel Borovikov)*

The next gun to be tested against the Tiger was another foreign gun: the 75 mm M3 mounted on the M4A2 Sherman tank. Two types of ammunition were tested: M72 shot fired at 600 m/s and an M61 shell fired at 564 m/s. The M61 shell scored a penetration against the side of the hull from 400 meters, breaking off a 300x300 mm piece of armor. This shell could also penetrate the 62 mm thick lower side armor from 650 m, knocking out a plug from the armor. A followup shot from the same range resulted in the same damage. M61 shells could not penetrate the upper side or the turret side at this range. Two shots with an M72 shot penetrated the side of the tank from 625 meters. Spalling was observed on the inside and outside.[63]

---

[63] TsAMO RF F.38 Op.11377 D.12 L.22-23

T-34 tank with an F-34 76 mm gun, Bovington Tank Museum. The T-34's gun proved ineffective against the Tiger's side and front armor. *(Peter Samsonov)*

The 76 mm F-34 gun used on the T-34 tank was next. Three AP shells were fired at 662 m/s at the upper side of the hull from a range of 650 meters, the side of the turret at 400 and at 200 meters. None of the three hits penetrated. Experimental HEAT, bicaliber[64], and solid shot rounds were also used in these trials, but only made dents in the Tiger's armor.[65]

A more powerful 76 mm gun achieved better results. The 76 mm 3-K model 1931 AA gun fired a 76 mm AP shell with a muzzle velocity of 815 m/s. This weapon was already considered obsolete and supplanted by the more powerful

---

[64] The term bicaliber refers to a weapon that can be converted to fire a different caliber by means of a different barrel or barrel insert. The report author almost certainly meant subcaliber.

[65] TsAMO RF F.38 Op.11377 D.12 L.25

85 mm 52-K, but nevertheless as of June 22nd, 1941, there were 3821 guns of this type in service compared to 2630 52-K.[66]

The 76 mm 3-K model 1931 AA gun penetrated the side of the turret from a range of 500 meters, breaking the weld seam holding the roof and deforming the roof by 50 mm. Two more shots at this range left only dents. Unlike most other shots fired in these trials, these were made at 30 degrees from normal. Another shot from 1000 m (this time at normal) also only left a dent, but a shot from 1450 m destroyed the weld seam at a length of 650 mm. A shot against the lower hull was also made at this range. The shell penetrated three road wheels but only left a dent in the armor.[67]

85 mm 52-K AA gun, Lenino-Snegiri. This 85 mm gun could be used both against air and ground targets. It proved to be an effective weapon against the Tiger's front and side armor even at long range. *(Pavel Borovikov)*

The next weapon to be tested was another AA gun, the 85 mm 52-K model 1939. This weapon proved itself to be effective against the Tiger's armor. A shot

---

[66] A. Shirokorad, *Artilleriya v Velikoy Otechestvennoy Voyne*, AST, Moscow, 2010, p.545
[67] TsAMO RF F.38 Op.11377 D.12 L.30

to the lower side (62 mm) from 800 meters made a 350x230 mm breach. One shot to the upper side from 1450 meters made a 110 mm wide hole with a 380 mm exit diameter. Considerable spalling was caused. A second shot made a 115 mm hole.[68]

The 52-K was the first weapon tested to successfully penetrate the front of the tank. From 1000 meters and at 30 degrees from normal, the gun made a hole 150 mm in diameter on entry and 160 mm on exit. There was considerable spalling and cracking of the lower front plate. Another shot at the lower front plate from 1500 meters landed near the previous penetration and cracked it into pieces. A shot to the upper front plate from 1500 meters did not penetrate.[69]

122 mm A-19 corps gun, Overloon War Museum. This was a powerful long range weapon designed to defeat tough fortifications. A hit from the A-19 was not only powerful enough to penetrate the armor, but to tear the Tiger's turret from its turret ring. *(Peter Samsonov)*

The next gun to be tested was the 122 mm A-19 model 1931 corps gun. Even though this was a field artillery piece that would be far too heavy to use as an

---

[68] TsAMO RF F.38 Op.11377 D.12 L.33
[69] TsAMO RF F.38 Op.11377 D.12 L.33-36

anti-tank gun, it had already been evaluated as a potential weapon against heavily armored targets back in 1941. The results were very promising, even with a concrete penetrating shell.[70] In 1943 this gun fired a B-471 AP shell at 800 m/s. The first shot made from 1500 meters aimed at the front of the tank, but passed through an opening previously made by the 85 mm gun. The shell went all the way through the Tiger and penetrated the rear armor, making a breach with an entrance diameter of 140 mm and exit diameter of 235 mm. Significant cracking was once again observed. The next shot fired from the same range hit the turret. It broke off a 580x230 mm chunk of armor, tore the turret off the turret ring, and moved it backwards by 540 mm. The third shot ricocheted off the roof of the Tiger, nevertheless sending several cracks through the plate.[71]

No satisfactory hits were scored by the 107 mm ZIS-6, 122 mm M-30, or 152 mm ML-20 during the trials, and therefore no conclusions were made about these systems.[72]

This was the end for artillery, but there were still some more weapons left to be tested. An experimental KB-30 HEAT grenade thrown at the tank could penetrate the 82 mm thick side armor, but only when it impacted at an angle close to 90 degrees.[73] A TMD-B mine with 5 kg TNT charge proved capable of severing the Tiger's track.[74] An experimental jumping mine produced at factory #627 also proved capable of penetrating the Tiger's 28 mm thick floor plate.[75]

---

[70] TsAMO RF F.38 Op.12104 D.261 L.7
[71] TsAMO RF F.38 Op.11377 D.12 L.37-38
[72] TsAMO RF F.38 Op.11377 D.12 L.1
[73] TsAMO RF F.38 Op.11377 D.12 L.42
[74] TsAMO RF F.38 Op.11377 D.12 L.45
[75] TsAMO RF F.38 Op.11377 D.12 L.46

Soviet infantrymen carrying a 14.5 mm PTRD anti-tank rifle at a reenactment at the Ontario Regiment Museum. Both this single shot rifle and the PTRS semiautomatic anti-tank rifles firing the same 14,5x114 mm cartridge were an effective weapon against light and even medium tanks, but were not powerful enough to penetrate the Tiger's armor. *(Peter Samsonov)*

Anti-tank rifles were also tested against the Tiger's armor. The PTRS firing a 14.5 mm bullet at a muzzle velocity of 1020 m/s could not penetrate the side armor. Neither could the experimental RES rifle (named after its three creators, Rashkov, Ermolayev, and Slukhotskiy) firing a 20 mm bullet at 1280 m/s or Blum 15P-2 rifle firing a 14.5 mm bullet at 1270 m/s. The Ostrovsky 70 mm HEAT launcher also failed to penetrate the armor. Only the Blum 43P rifle had any success. The 1500 m/s muzzle velocity of a 14.5 mm bullet fired from a necked down 23 mm aircraft gun casing penetrated not just the lower 62 mm thick side, but also the upper 82 mm thick side (albeit inconsistently).[76]

Two passes were made at the Tiger from aircraft. A LAG-3 fighter with a 37 mm gun scored three hits out of 35 shots fired, penetrating the roof. An IL-2

---

[76] TsAMO RF F.38 Op.11377 D.12 L.47-52

ground attack aircraft scored three hits out of 55 with the same weapon. Two hits penetrated the tracks, but did not sever them.[77]

The conclusions of the report listed the following weapons as effective measures against the Tiger tank:

- 85 mm 52-K AA gun against the front armor at ranges of up to 1000 meters and against the side armor at 1500 meters.
- The British 6-pounder and Soviet 57 mm ZIS-2 against the side armor at ranges of up to 1000 meters.
- The American 75 mm M3 gun against the side armor at ranges of up to 650 meters.
- The 45 mm model 1942 anti-tank gun against the side armor at up to 350 meters.
- The KB-30 HEAT grenade and 37 mm aircraft cannon against the roof of the tank.

The report also noted that AP and HE from any gun 57 mm or bigger in caliber aimed at the tracks and running gear would stop the tank, as would the existing TMD-B mine.[78]

The armor of the tank was brittle despite its medium hardness (241-302 BHN). It cracked and spalled when hit with 57, 85, and 122 mm shells. The weld seams were also brittle and were destroyed by impacts from AP shells.[79]

Data discovered in this trial was composed into a penetration diagram and distributed to troops on May 23rd, 1943.[80]

Next page: A diagram summarizing weapons and ranges that could defeat the Tiger tank distributed to Soviet troops. *(Peter Samsonov)*

---

[77] TsAMO RF F.38 Op.11377 D.12 L.53-54
[78] TsAMO RF F.38 Op.11377 D.12 L.59
[79] TsAMO RF F.38 Op.11377 D.12 L.58
[80] Y. Pasholok, *Bey chem popalo*, https://yuripasholok.livejournal.com/12451720.html, retrieved on January 23rd, 2024

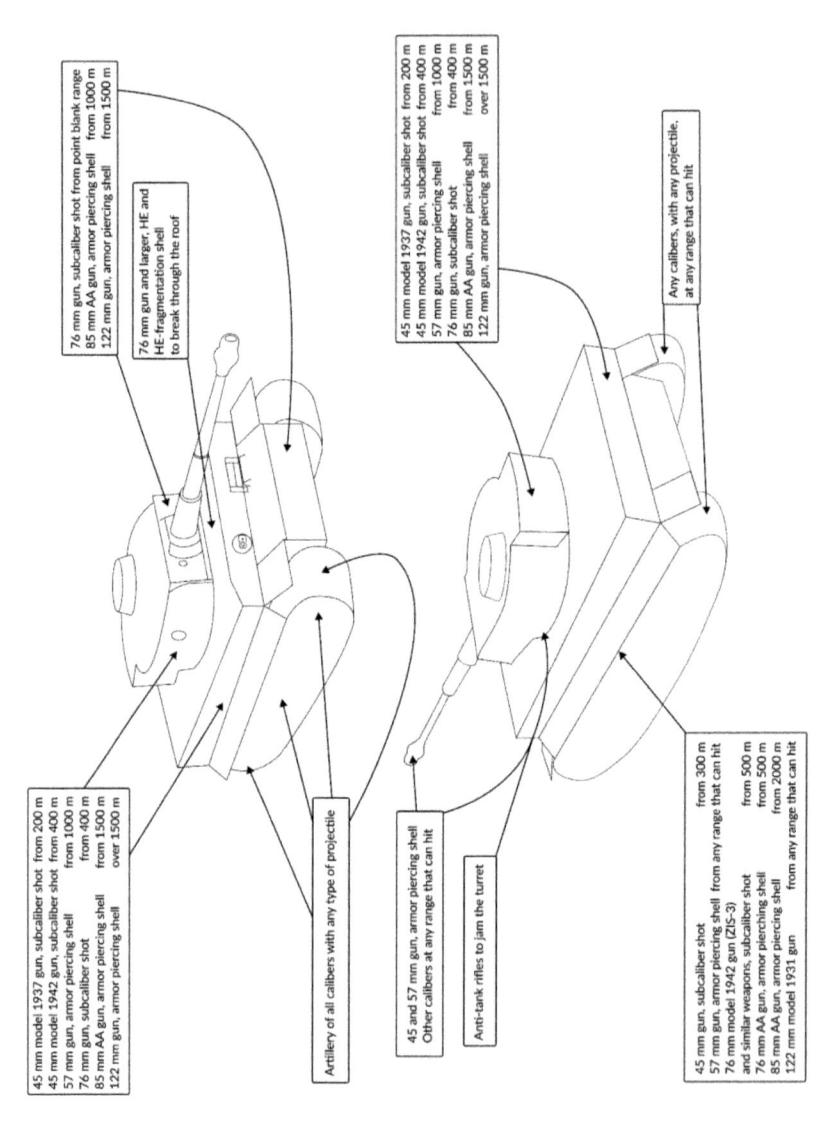

Callout (upper left turret):
76 mm gun, subcaliber shot from point blank range
45 mm AA gun, armor piercing shell from 1000 m
122 mm gun, armor piercing shell from 1500 m

Callout (turret roof):
76 mm gun and larger, HE and HE-fragmentation shell to break through the roof

Callout (upper right turret):
45 mm model 1937 gun, subcaliber shot from 200 m
45 mm model 1942 gun, subcaliber shot from 400 m
57 mm gun, armor piercing shell from 1000 m
76 mm gun, subcaliber shot from 400 m
85 mm AA gun, armor piercing shell from 1500 m
122 mm gun, armor piercing shell over 1500 m

Callout (right side):
Any calibers, with any projectile, at any range that can hit

Callout (lower left hull):
45 mm model 1937 gun, subcaliber shot from 200 m
45 mm model 1942 gun, subcaliber shot from 400 m
57 mm gun, armor piercing shell from 1000 m
76 mm gun, subcaliber shot from 400 m
85 mm AA gun, armor piercing shell from 1500 m
122 mm gun, armor piercing shell over 1500 m

Callout (hull side):
Artillery of all calibers with any type of projectile

Callout (hull front):
45 and 57 mm gun, armor piercing shell from any range that can hit
Other calibers at any range that can hit

Callout (gun barrel):
Anti-tank rifles to jam the turret

Callout (lower right):
45 mm gun, subcaliber shot from 300 m
57 mm gun, armor piercing shell from any range that can hit
76 mm model 1942 gun (ZIS-3) and similar weapons, subcaliber shot from 500 m
76 mm AA gun, armor piercing shell from 500 m
85 mm AA gun, armor piercing shell from 2000 m
122 mm model 1931 gun from any range that can hit

Elements of the German T-VI tank that can be reliably defeated by our artillery

Guns to Kill a Tiger

Despite having found weapons that were effective against the Tiger, the report was still concerning. The problem was that the 76 mm gun used by T-34 medium and KV-1 heavy tanks was ineffective against this new opponent with any type of ammunition available at the time. The 57 mm ZIS-2 gun was taken out of production back in 1941. Only 10 T-34 tanks with the ZIS-4 (tank variant of the ZIS-2) were built. While the 85 mm 52-K and 122 mm A-19 were still in use, they were far too large to mount in a tank turret.

A number of solutions were ordered as a result of these trials. One direction ordered by the GABTU (*Glavnoye Avto-Bronetankovoye Upravleniye*, Main Auto-Armour Directorate) was improvement of existing weapons. A new type of AP shell capable of penetrating the side of the Tiger from 600 meters and a subcaliber AP shot capable of penetrating the front from 500 meters were needed. Even the performance of the 85 mm 52-K was unsatisfactory. A shell capable of penetrating 100-110 mm of armor from 2000 meters was ordered.

The 57 mm gun project was dusted off as well. 20-30% of T-34 tanks should be built with 57 mm guns according to these new plans. An order for new 57 mm HE ammunition was also made. The 57 mm gun would also be installed in the SU-76 SPG to make it into a potent tank destroyer. Two more tank destroyers would be built, one on the T-34 chassis with an 85 mm gun and one on the SU-152 chassis with a 122 mm A-19 gun (not to be confused with the SU-122, which used the lower velocity 122 mm M-30 howitzer). Development of a 100 mm tank gun was also ordered at this stage.[81]

It is interesting to note that few of these initiatives worked out as intended. While four T-34 tanks with 57 mm ZIS-4 guns were built in 1943, they only took part in trials in July-August 1943. No large batch was ordered, as the power of

---

[81] TsAMO RF F.38 Op.11355 D.1380 L.187-188

the weapon was no longer considered sufficient after the Battle of Kursk.[82] A 76 mm gun with the ballistics of the 76 mm 3-K AA gun used in these trials was also tested in the turret of a T-34 tank. This was a more powerful weapon that could penetrate 90 mm of armor at an angle of 30 degrees with AP ammunition and up to 160 mm of armor with tungsten core subcaliber shot. This weapon was not put into mass production either.[83] A major reason for this was that the 85 mm S-53 gun with the ballistics of the 52-K AA gun could also fit in the turret of a T-34 tank. This weapon was tested and even accepted into production. However, a parallel development of the T-43 tank also gave the Red Army a larger 3-man turret with a 1600 mm wide turret ring. It turned out to be much easier to operate an 85 mm gun in the enlarged turret, and so the T-34-85 went into production instead of the regular T-34 with a larger gun.[84] The T-34 with the 76 mm F-34 gun had to make do with a new tungsten core subcaliber AP shot. It could penetrate up to 92 mm of armor at 500 meters, meaning that the shot fell short of the requirements outlined by the GABTU. However, it could penetrate up to 110 mm of armor at 300 meters and 128 mm at 100 meters, meaning that the T-34 could penetrate the front of a Tiger at a closer range.[85]

Work on a tank destroyer armed with a 57 mm gun on the chassis of the SU-76 only began in April of 1944. By this point, the SU-76 was out of production and the SU-76M was used as a chassis. The conversion was not difficult since the ZIS-2 and ZIS-3 had a common carriage and trials were performed on May 1st-4th, 1944. A second improved prototype completed trials on July 30th. Work went on as far as drafting a decree for the State Committee of Defense (GOKO) to accept the vehicle into production as the SU-57. Unfortunately, by that point the penetration of the 57 mm gun was no longer considered satisfactory and the SU-57 never entered production.[86]

---

[82] Y. Pasholok, *Teoriya bronetankovykh zabluzhdeniy: seredina Velikoy Otechestvennoy*, https://warspot.ru/16316-teoriya-bronetankovyh-zabluzhdeniy-seredina-velikoy-otechestvennoy, retrieved on October 29th, 2023

[83] Y. Pasholok, *Poslednee prishestviye 76-mm dyrokola*, https://dzen.ru/media/yuripasholok/poslednee-prishestvie-76mm-dyrokola-615656c882810e092430e260, retrieved on October 29th, 2023

[84] Y. Pasholok, *Pushki pobolshe dlya T-34 ili kak pytatsya v zaitsa zapikhnut' utku*, https://dzen.ru/media/yuripasholok/pushki-pobolshe-dlia-t34-ili-kak-pytatsia-v-zaica-zapihnut-utku-5f914951c2b29d2294eca2b0, retrieved on October 29th, 2023

[85] TsAMO RF F.1233 Op.1 D.152 L.52

[86] Y. Pasholok, *Lyogkiye SAU s bolshimi pushkami*, https://warspot.ru/12623-lyogkie-sau-s-bolshimi-pushkami, retrieved on October 29th, 2023

ISU-122 tank destroyer, Museum of National Military History, Padikovo. This was not a high priority project and it took almost a year to put a heavy tank destroyer into production. *(Pavel Borovikov)*

Like the SU-57, work on a tank destroyer with a 122 mm A-19 gun was of lower priority and by the time it began the SU-152 was out of production. It was replaced by the ISU-152 on the chassis of the IS tank, and so the gun was installed on the new vehicle. This also required few modifications, since the 152 mm ML-20 and 122 mm A-19 shared a carriage. The Object 241 (ISU-152 prototype) was chosen for conversion. The new vehicle was designated Object 242. Work began in December of 1943 and trials were completed by the end of the year. Priority of this project remained low and Stalin only signed the order to accept the Object 242 into service under the name ISU-122 on March 12th, 1944.[87]

Stalin prioritized work on a medium tank destroyer armed with an 85 mm gun. GKO decree #3289ss ordering the development of such a vehicle was signed

---

[87] Y. Pasholok, *Tyazheliy istrebitel' tankov*, https://warspot.ru/14162-tyazhyolyy-istrebitel-tankov, retrieved on October 29th, 2023

on May 5th, 1943. Despite the GABTU's preference for a tank destroyer with a rear casemate, the decree explicitly stated that the chassis of the SU-122 with a frontal casemate was to be used.[88] Fortunately, 85 mm guns for Soviet tank destroyers were nothing new. Work on a tank destroyer with an 85 mm gun began back in 1940. Factory #8 was tasked with adapting the 85 mm 52-K AA gun for installation in a turret installed on the hull of an A-42 tractor based on the T-34 chassis. This project was not successful.[89] However, this was not the end. Factory #8 continued their work on 85 mm guns after evacuation to the Urals. Work on a gun called ZIK-1 began in March of 1941. This gun could be installed in the turret of a KV-1 or T-34 tank. The project was also rejected, but the 85 mm gun got another chance at life with the discovery of the Tiger tank. Factory #9 (a factory specializing in tank guns split off from factory #8)[90] developed an 85 mm gun with the ballistics of the 52-K AA gun for installation into a tank destroyer. This gun was designated D-5.[91] Design work was completed by May 26th, 1943, and a prototype of a new tank destroyer was delivered for trials on July 25th, 1943.[92] The vehicle was accepted into service under the name SU-85 on August 8th, 1943, by GKO decree #3892.[93] Production of the SU-85 began in late August and delivered 100 SU-85 tank destroyers by September 1st, 1943, and the first SPG regiment equipped with the SU-85 was in the field by October.[94]

---

[88] RGASPI F.644 Op.2 D.165 L.88

[89] Y. Pasholok, *Sovetskiye Istrebiteli Tankov s Krugovym Obstrelom*, https://warspot.ru/4819-u-20-sovetskie-istrebiteli-tankov-s-krugovym-obstrelom, retrieved on October 30th, 2023

[90] RGASPI F.644 Op.2 D.105 L.24

[91] TsAMO RF F.81 Op.12063 D.19 L.155-156

[92] Y. Pasholok, *Put' ot srednego shturmovika k srednemu istrebitelyu*, https://warspot.ru/10662-put-ot-srednego-shturmovika-k-srednemu-istrebitelyu, retrieved on October 30th, 2023

[93] RGASPI F.644 Op.2 D.202 L.139

[94] Y. Pasholok, *Dolgozhdanniy istrebitel'*, https://warspot.ru/11413-dolgozhdannyy-istrebitel, retrieved on October 31st, 2023

SU-85 tank destroyer, Museum of National Military History, Padikovo. The fastest way to obtain a new tank destroyer was to modify the SU-122 chassis to take a high velocity 85 mm gun. *(Pavel Borovikov)*

Decree #3289ss also instructed factory #9 to develop an 85 mm gun for use in a heavy tank.[95] This was no surprise, as the newest heavy tank in development at the Kirov Factory in Chelyabinsk (ChKZ) was still armed with a 76 mm gun.[96] This gun was initially designated D-7, but was later renamed D-5T-85 as it was essentially a tank variant of the tank destroyer weapon. Similarly, the D-5 was renamed D-5S-85.[97] The D-5T-85 gun was installed into a new tank called Object 237.[98] In order to get a heavy tank with an 85 mm gun in the field faster, there was another heavy tank built with the D-5T-85: the Object 239. The Object 239 consisted of a modified KV-1S chassis with a widened turret ring to accept the turret from the Object 237.[99] The Object 239 was accepted into service as the KV-85 on August 8th, 1943, by GKO decree #3891.[100] The first

---

[95] RGASPI F.644 Op.2 D.165 L.88
[96] RGASPI F.644 Op.2 D.138 L.194-196
[97] TsAMO RF F.81 Op.12063 D.19 L.155-156
[98] TsAMO RF F.38 Op.11355 D.1377 L.195
[99] Y. Pasholok, *Kutsak Kotina*, https://warspot.ru/10800-kutsak-kotina, retrieved on October 31st, 2023
[100] RGASPI F.644 Op.2 D.202 L.135

16 KV-85 tanks were delivered by August 31st, 1943, and the first shipment of tanks was made on September 23rd. KV-85 tanks were issued to units already armed with the KV-1S and familiar with the chassis.[101]

The KV-85 was only a temporary measure. Decree #4043 accepted the Object 237 into service under the name IS on September 4th, 1943.[102] Delivery of these tanks began in November of 1943 and the heavy tank regiments received their first IS tanks in December.[103] More details on the development of IS-1 and IS-2 tanks and the Tiger tank's influence on their designs can be found in the author's book on the subject: *IS-2: Development, Design & Production of Stalin's War Hammer*, Military History Group, 2023.

The technique of combining a new turret carrying the 85 mm D-5T-85 gun and an existing chassis was repeated with the T-34-85. This vehicle was accepted into service by GKO decree #4776 on December 15th, 1943.[104] Unlike the KV-85, the T-34-85 was here to stay, although the D-5T-85 was quickly replaced with the more compact ZIS-S-53 that also had the ballistics of the 85 mm 52-K AA gun. Production of the T-34-85 began in January of 1944.[105] T-34-85 tanks were first used in combat in March of 1944.[106]

As one can see, the reaction to the Tiger was swift once the vehicles were tested. Thanks to a combination of existing weapons and chassis, the Red Army was able to field vehicles (see table) that were capable of successfully engaging Tiger tanks at long range a mere five months after penetration trials were completed. At first these were specialized vehicles such as heavy tanks and tank destroyers, but it was not long before the Red Army's medium tank received a gun capable of effectively fighting a heavy tank that weighed almost twice as

---

[101] Y. Pasholok, *Kutsak Kotina*, https://warspot.ru/10800-kutsak-kotina, retrieved on October 31st, 2023
[102] RGASPI F.644 Op.2 D.211 L.1
[103] Y. Pasholok, *Promezhutochniy IS*, https://warspot.ru/11074-promezhutochnyy-is, retrieved on May 22nd, 2021
[104] RGASPI F.644 Op.2 D.252 L.140
[105] RGASPI F.644 Op.2 D.255 L.104
[106] Park Patriot, *Sredniy Tank T-34-85*, https://parkpatriot.ru/o-parke/tekhnika-parka/sredniy-tank-t-34-85_Tex_centr, retrieved on October 31st, 2023

much. This tank was produced in great numbers, and by the end of April of 1944, there were more T-34 tanks equipped with a gun capable of knocking out a Tiger at long range than the total number of Tiger tanks built.[107] An improved 85 mm armor piercing shell with improved penetration was also developed and issued starting in January of 1944, enabling them to defeat the Tiger from a greater range.[108]

The 85 mm 52-K gun was not the full extent of "Tiger killers" built by the Red Army. As noted above, one of the weapons identified to be effective against the Tiger was the 122 mm A-19 corps gun. However, this was a heavy weapon that was entirely unsuitable for use as an anti-tank gun. GKO decree #3290ss ordered the development of a new lighter weapon: a corps gun with the ballistics of the 100 mm B-34 naval gun (muzzle velocity of 900 m/s, 15.6 kg shell, maximum range 22 km).[109] A tank gun based on this weapon was pitched back in 1941 by the Kirov Factory in Leningrad, but turned down at the time as land artillery did not use the 100 mm caliber and no AP shell was available for it.[110] The development of a 100 mm field gun was the perfect time to realize the GABTU's requirement for a 100 mm tank gun with the same ballistics.

---

[107] M. Kolomiyets, *T-34 Pervaya polnaya entsiklopediya*, Yauza, Moscow, 2009, p.484
[108] M. Kolomiyets, *T-34 Pervaya polnaya entsiklopediya*, Yauza, Moscow, 2009. p.453
[109] RGASPI F.644 Op.2 D.156 L.92
[110] TsAMO RF F.81 Op.12104 D.201 L.11-12

T-34-85 tank, Overloon War Museum. Most T-34-85 tanks mounted the ZIS-S-53 85 mm gun, a more compact weapon with the same ballistics as the D-5T-85. This tank gave even ordinary tank units the ability to destroy Tiger tanks without waiting for help from heavy tanks or tank destroyers. *(Peter Samsonov)*

Name	Date accepted into service	Weapon	Description
SU-85	Aug 8th, 1943	85 mm D-5S	Tank destroyer based on the chassis of the SU-122 SPG.
KV-85	Aug 8th, 1943	85 mm D-5T	Heavy tank based on the KV-1S chassis with a widened turret ring and the turret of an IS-1 tank.
IS-1	Sept 4th, 1943	85 mm D-5T	New heavy tank design developed from the ground up with armor capable of resisting the Tiger's gun.
IS-2	Oct 31st, 1943	122 mm D-25T	IS-1 chassis and turret with a more powerful 122 mm gun installed.
T-34	Not accepted	57 mm ZIS-4	T-34 tank equipped with a high velocity 57 mm gun, similar to the tanks built in 1941. 4 experimental vehicles were built.
T-34	Not accepted	76 mm S-54	T-34 tank equipped with a tank version of the 76 mm 3-K AA gun. 1 experimental vehicle was built.
T-34-85	Dec 15th, 1943	85 mm D-5T	T-34 tank with a wider turret ring, new enlarged turret, and an 85 mm gun.
	Jan 1st, 1944	85 mm ZIS-S-53	

Vehicles developed in 1943 armed with a gun capable of penetrating the Tiger's front armor.

SU-100 tank destroyer, Museum of National Military History, Padikovo. Installation of a 100 mm gun on a modernized SU-85 gave the Red Army a tank destroyer that could defeat Tiger tanks at great range. *(Pavel Borovikov)*

Factory #9 developed a gun designated D-10. As with the D-5, there were two versions of it: the D-10T for installation into tanks and D-10S for installation into tank destroyers. The D-10T was tested in the IS-4 tank (Object 245, not to be confused with the Object 701 developed much later) in April of 1944.[111] Ultimately, the superior penetration and HE-fragmentation effect of the 122 mm D-25T was found to be preferable for heavy tanks, but the D-10T could be recommended for use in medium tanks.[112] The tank destroyer variant was much more successful. Work on a tank destroyer with a 100 mm gun began in February of 1944. The SU-85 chassis was taken as the starting point. A prototype was put through trials in March. Even though conclusions were very positive, a second improved prototype was built and tested from June 24th to

---

[111] TsAMO RF F.38 Op.11369 D.28 L.17-17 (reverse)
[112] TsAMO RF F.38 Op.11369 D.490 L.37-38

June 27th, 1944.[113] The SU-100 was accepted into service on July 3rd, 1944, by GKO decree #6131.[114]

IS-2 heavy tank, Museum of National Military History, Padikovo. At a much lower weight than the Tiger, the IS-2 had enough armor to withstand a hit from the 88 mm KwK 36 gun and knock out the Tiger in return at a range of over two kilometers. *(Pavel Borovikov)*

An important event took place shortly after the order to develop new weapons to defeat the Tiger tank. The Red Army discovered two new types of heavily armored German AFVs at the Battle of Kursk during the summer of 1943: the Panther and the Ferdinand. Trials showed that the 85 mm gun was ineffective against the sloped frontal armor of the Panther tank. Trials held between December 1st and 14th, 1943, showed that the newly adopted 85 mm

---

[113] Y. Pasholok, *Optimalnaya modernizatsiya*, https://warspot.ru/13911-optimalnaya-modernizatsiya, retrieved on November 1st, 2023

[114] RGASPI F.644 Op.2 D.349 L.43

D-5 gun was ineffective against the upper front plate at any range.[115] This was not a surprise. A commission sent to study the battlefield at Kursk in July of 1943 examined 23 knocked out Panthers and found few with penetrations of the upper front plate. Field trials conducted with 45 mm and 76 mm guns as well as 122 mm howitzers confirmed that the front armor of the tank was very strong.[116] Thankfully, trials held against the Tiger tank in April of 1943 already revealed that the Red Army had a reserve of potential anti-tank weapons. A shortened barrel of the 122 mm A-19 gun equipped with a muzzle brake could be combined with elements already developed for the 85 mm D-5 to create a powerful 122 mm tank gun. A draft project for installation of this gun was ready by July 14th, 1943, long before factory #9 would have found out any information about the Panther tank.[117] GKO decree #4043 that accepted the IS tank into production also ordered the installation of this new gun (now named D-25) into the new heavy tank.[118] The resulting tank known as IS-122 or IS-2 was accepted into service on October 31st, 1943.[119] The first IS-2 tanks were built in November of 1943[120] and arrived on the front lines on February 15th, 1944.[121] Therefore, thanks to the early warning given by the appearance of Tiger tanks, Soviet tanks capable of defeating the Panther at long range were deployed just two months after the conclusion of penetration trials that confirmed that the 122 mm D-25T gun could defeat a Panther tank at a range of over 2 kilometers.[122]

Testing the Tiger's Gun

While Tiger #100 was being shot up, Tiger #121 was used for gunnery trials. A KV-1 tank was chosen as its target, placed at a range of 1500 meters. The first shot hit the front of the hull, bounced upwards and only left a dent in the 30

---

[115] Y. Pasholok, *Strashnee koshki zverya net*, https://warspot.ru/11907-strashnee-koshki-zverya-net, retrieved on November 1st, 2023

[116] M. Svirin, *Tyazheliy tank Pantera Pz.Kpfw V*, Tseyghaus, Moscow, 2007, pp.20-24

[117] Y. Pasholok, *IS s Tyazhelym Vooruzheniyev*, https://warspot.ru/11233-is-s-tyazhyolym-vooruzheniem, retrieved on November 1st, 2023

[118] RGASPI F.644 Op.2 D.211 L.1

[119] RGASPI F.644 Op.2 D.239 L.101

[120] Y. Pasholok, *Borba za mesto na konveyere*, https://warspot.ru/11457-borba-za-mesto-na-konveyere, retrieved on November 1st, 2023

[121] M. Svirin, *Tyazheliye tanki IS*, Tseyghaus, Moscow, 2007, p.32

[122] TsAMO RF F.38 Op.11355 D.2375 L.3-4

mm thick applique armor plate. The main 75 mm thick hull armor was not damaged. A second shot at the same portion of the armor was much more effective. The AP shell went through both the applique armor and the main armor, making a breach 110x130 mm in size at the entrance and 180x210 mm in size at the exit. A 230x210 piece of the applique armor was also broken off. Two cracks opened up on the applique armor. The third shot made to the hull was with an HE shell, which broke off a part of the applique armor weakened by the previous hit.[123]

Two more shots were fired at the back of the turret (the KV-1's gun was turned backwards during trials). Both shots penetrated. The first made a breach 120x110 mm at the entrance and 190x130 mm at the exit. The second made a 110x90 mm breach.[124]

A T-34 tank was shot up with similar results. The first shot fired at a range of 1500 meters hit the turret ring, displacing the turret. The rest of the shots were aimed at the hull. The first ricocheted off the driver's hatch, knocking it into the hull. The second made a 160x90 mm breach in the armor and created several cracks. The third hit the cast beam connecting the upper and lower front plates, making a breach with an entrance size of 90x90 mm and exit of 200x100 mm. A crack also formed in the welds holding the beam in place. The final shot was an HE shell that only formed a small dent in the upper front plate but cracked the weld seam between the plate and the side armor.[125]

Interestingly enough, the Soviet 85 mm 52-K AA gun was also used in these trials. The gun showed similar effectiveness to the Tiger's 88 mm Kwk 36 against T-34 and KV-1 hulls when tested at a range of 1500 meters.[126] This is not surprising, as the 52-K and the 88 mm Flak 36 gun that the KwK 36 was based on shared a common ancestor and evolved along similar lines.[127] In addition to concluding that the German 88 mm gun can penetrate the front armor of a T-

---

[123] TsAMO RF F.38 Op.11355 D.1545 L.9-10
[124] TsAMO RF F.38 Op.11355 D.1545 L.9
[125] M. Kolomiyets, *T-34 Pervaya polnaya entsiklopediya*, Yauza, Moscow, 2009. p.452
[126] TsAMO RF F.38 Op.11355 D.1545 L.17
[127] Y. Pasholok, *Tyazheliy Trofey*, https://warspot.ru/9797-tyazhyolyy-trofey, retrieved on October 26th, 2023

34 and a KV-1 tank at 1500 meters, the report also states that the 52-K gun has similar power to the German 88 mm gun and can be used effectively to combat enemy tanks. The report also concluded that 88 mm HE does not destroy Soviet tanks and deals insignificant damage when it hits their armor, but this was little consolation.[128]

The Tiger's 88 mm KwK 36 gun and its ammunition, Musée des Blindés, Saumur. This gun was a powerful weapon capable of knocking out both the T-34 and the KV-1 at a long range. *(Peter Samsonov)*

Unlike the armor penetration trials, the results of gunnery trials brought few surprises. The Red Army already knew about the armor penetrating power of German AA guns before the war and prepared accordingly. The Red Army was aware of a 88 mm AA gun firing a 9 kg shell at a muzzle velocity of 820 m/s. This gun was known to penetrate 90 mm of armor at a range of up to 1300 m at normal and up to 700 m at an angle of 30 degrees. By May of 1941, Red Army intelligence was aware of an "88 mm heavy anti-tank gun" firing a 10.2 kg shell

---

[128] M. Kolomiyets, *T-34 Pervaya polnaya entsiklopediya*, Yauza, Moscow, 2009. p.452

at 850 m/s, penetrating up to 100 mm of armor.[129] Intelligence was supplemented by real trials, as the USSR managed to purchase a 10.5 cm Flak 39 AA gun from Germany in 1940. 130 mm of armor was considered to provide adequate defense against this weapon.[130] Soviet heavy tanks proposed in 1941 were adequately protected from German guns. The KV-3 would have 120 mm of front armor that would give it decent protection against the 88 mm AA gun and the KV-4 would have 130 mm thick front armor that would protect it from the heavier 105 mm gun.[131] The shape of the hull remained the same as on the KV-1, presenting the armor at a 30 degree slope.[132] No prototype of either vehicle was ever completed due to the invasion of the USSR by Germany in the summer of 1941.

Although the KV-3 never made it into mass production, 120 mm thick armor sloped at 30 degrees remained the desired level of protection for a heavy tank. The IS-1 (blueprint #233) and IS-2 (blueprint #234) approved by GKO decree #2943 on February 24th, 1943, had this much armor.[133] When the trials of captured Tiger tanks revealed that the 76 mm gun used on the IS-1 was no longer sufficient, Stalin gave the order to install an 85 mm gun in the new heavy tank.[134] However, the requirements for armor remained the same, and the IS-1 (Object 237) accepted into service by GKO decree #4043 on September 4th, 1943, had the same level of armor: 120 mm at 30 degrees.[135] The IS-2 (Object 240) accepted into service on October 31st, 1943, had the same level of armor.[136] The IS-2's armor was only improved in March of 1944 as a reaction to the higher penetrating guns used by the Panther tank and Ferdinand tank destroyer.[137] The requirement for protection against the 88 mm Flak 36 gun set back in 1941 resulted in the development of a tank capable of withstanding fire

---

[129] TsAMO RF F.38 Op.11353 D.951 L.1
[130] Y. Pasholok, *Tankostroyeniye na grani zdravogo smysla*, https://warspot.ru/4995-tankostroenie-na-grani-zdravogo-smysla, retrieved on November 2nd, 2023
[131] TsAMO RF F.38 Op.11355 D.949 L.1
[132] Y. Pasholok, *KV-3: Nabor tankovoy massy*, https://warspot.ru/4960-kv-3-nabor-tankovoy-massy, retrieved on November 3rd, 2023
[133] RGASPI F.644 Op.2 D.138 L.194-195
[134] RGASPI F.644 Op.2 D.165 L.88
[135] RGASPI F.644 Op.2 D.211 L.1
[136] RGASPI F.644 Op.2 D.239 L.101
[137] M. Postnikov, *Bronezaschita Tyazhelikh Tankov KV i IS 1941-1945*, Eksprint, Moscow, 2006, p.28-29

from the Tiger's 88 mm Kwk 36 even before the Red Army knew about Tiger tanks.

Next page: Calculated penetration values of the 8.8 cm KwK 36 against the T-34 tank (translated from German). Solid black indicates areas where penetration is likely from the distance indicated, hashed areas indicate areas where a hit would degrade the performance of the tank, but not necessarily destroy it. The letter codes were invented by the Germans to distinguish between different variants of Soviet tanks and were not official Red Army designations. "T-34 A" represents the basic T-34 model as produced in the spring-summer of 1941, "T-34 B" represents a vehicle with a cast turret and thicker front armor produced in early 1942. *(Peter Samsonov)*[138]

---

[138] *Anlage zu H.Dv. 469/3b Panzer-Beschußtafel 8,8 cm KwK 36 as published on February 15th, 1943*

26-ton T 34 A Medium Panzer

Front

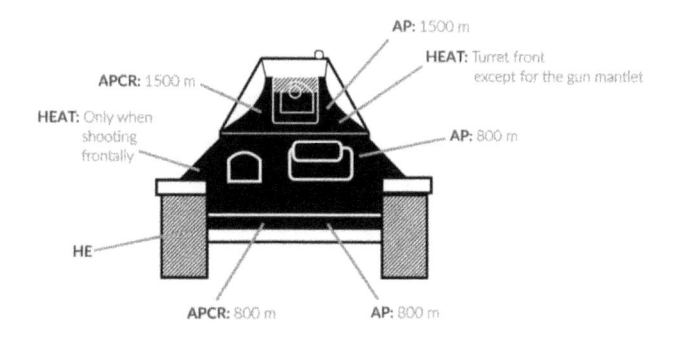

AP: 1500 m
HEAT: Turret front except for the gun mantlet
APCR: 1500 m
HEAT: Only when shooting frontally
AP: 800 m
HE
APCR: 800 m
AP: 800 m

Side

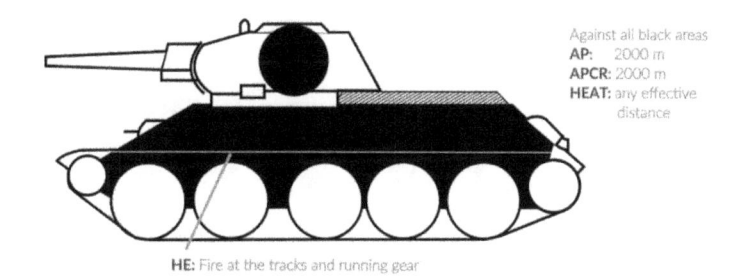

Against all black areas
AP: 2000 m
APCR: 2000 m
HEAT: any effective distance

HE: Fire at the tracks and running gear

Rear

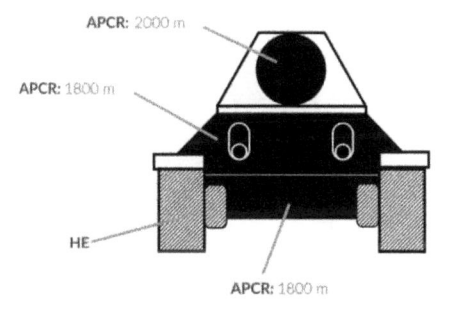

APCR: 2000 m
APCR: 1800 m
Against all black areas
AP: 2000 m
HEAT: any effective distance
HE
APCR: 1800 m

26-ton T 34 B Medium Panzer (reinforced)

Front

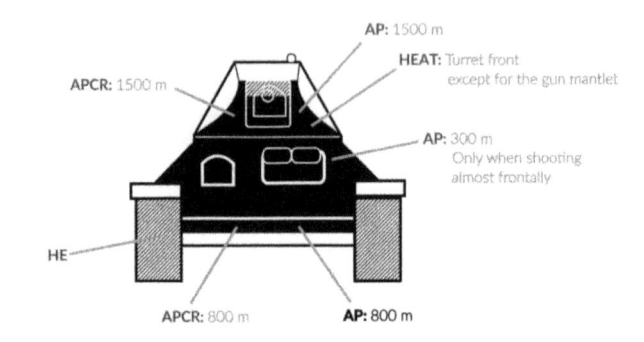

APCR: 1500 m

AP: 1500 m

HEAT: Turret front except for the gun mantlet

AP: 300 m
Only when shooting almost frontally

HE

APCR: 800 m

AP: 800 m

Side

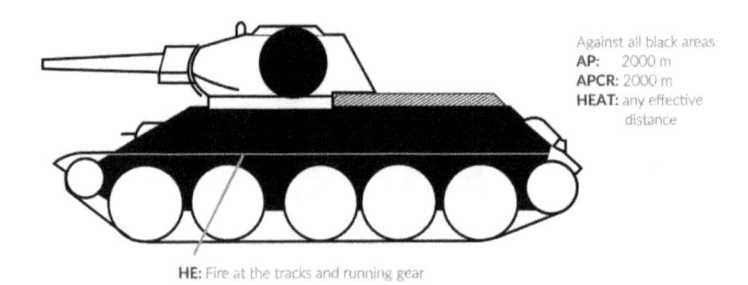

Against all black areas
AP: 2000 m
APCR: 2000 m
HEAT: any effective distance

HE: Fire at the tracks and running gear

Rear

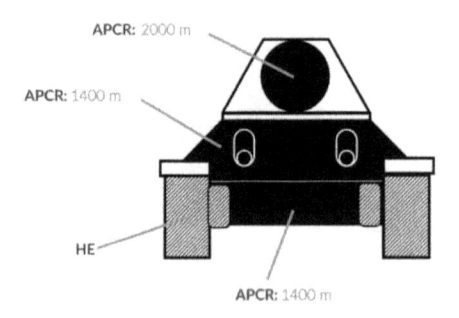

APCR: 2000 m

APCR: 1400 m

Against all black areas
AP: 2000 m
HEAT: any effective distance

HE

APCR: 1400 m

44-ton KV I A Heavy Panzer

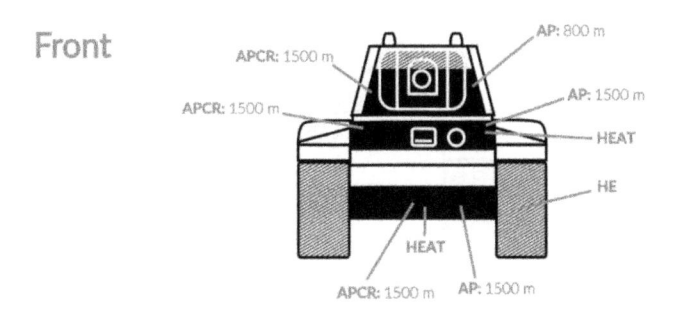

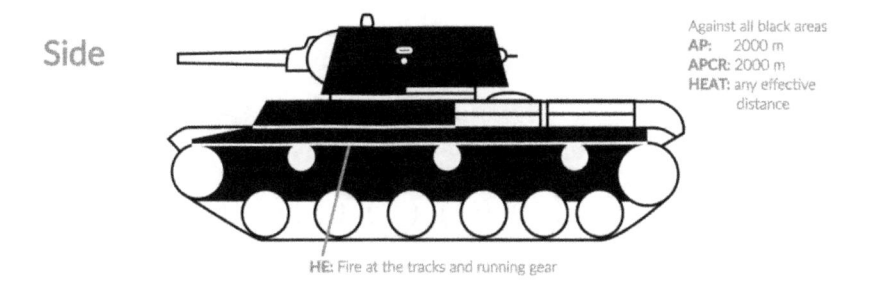

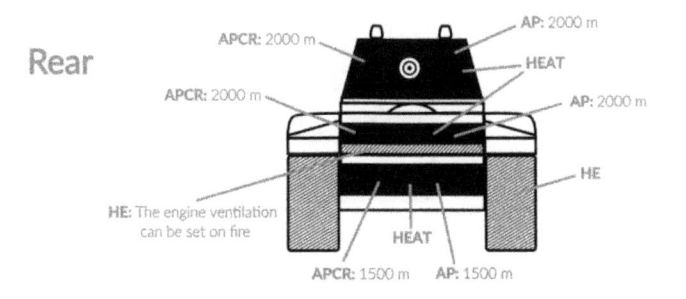

Front

APCR: 1500 m
APCR: 1500 m
AP: 800 m
AP: 1500 m
HEAT
HE
HEAT
APCR: 1500 m
AP: 1500 m

Side

Against all black areas
AP: 2000 m
APCR: 2000 m
HEAT: any effective distance

HE: Fire at the tracks and running gear

Rear

APCR: 2000 m
APCR: 2000 m
AP: 2000 m
HEAT
AP: 2000 m
HE
HE: The engine ventilation can be set on fire
HEAT
APCR: 1500 m
AP: 1500 m

44-ton KV I C Heavy Panzer (reinforced)

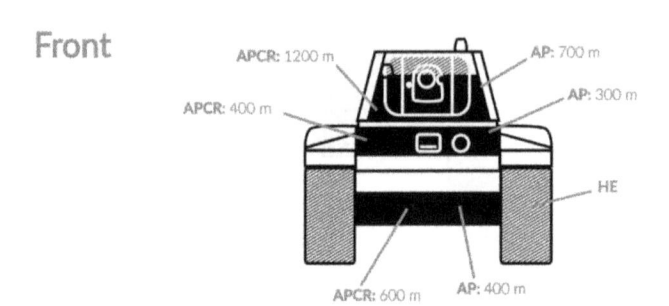

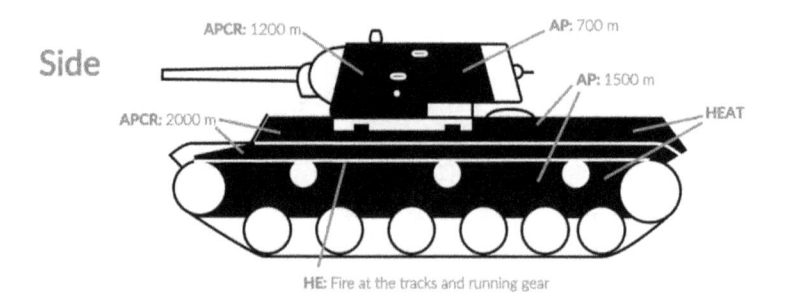

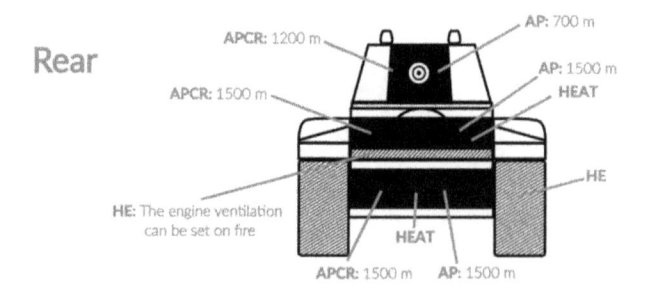

Front

APCR: 1200 m
APCR: 400 m
AP: 700 m
AP: 300 m
HE
APCR: 600 m
AP: 400 m

Side

APCR: 1200 m
AP: 700 m
AP: 1500 m
APCR: 2000 m
HEAT

HE: Fire at the tracks and running gear

Rear

APCR: 1200 m
AP: 700 m
AP: 1500 m
APCR: 1500 m
HEAT
HE
HE: The engine ventilation can be set on fire
HEAT
APCR: 1500 m
AP: 1500 m

Previous page: Calculated penetration values of the 8.8 cm KwK 36 against the KV-1 tank (translated from German). Solid black indicates areas where penetration is likely from the distance indicated, hashed areas indicate areas where a hit would degrade the performance of the tank, but not necessarily destroy it. The letter codes were invented by the Germans to distinguish between different variants of Soviet tanks and were not official Red Army designations. The "KV-1A" represents an early KV-1 tank with an L-11 gun, the "KV-1C" represents a later tank with a ZIS-5 gun and thicker armor. *(Peter Samsonov)*[139]

The German Reaction

As it could be expected, German intelligence was keeping an eye on its enemy's anti-tank capabilities. A memo circulated by the OKH on October 30th, 1943, shed some light on their reaction to the new Soviet developments. Interestingly enough, even though the report is clearly based on Soviet penetration trials carried out above, the data is slightly different. In some cases, additional data is present. Unfortunately, the author has not to date encountered the Soviet document(s) where these values were taken from.

As discovered in Soviet penetration trials, the Tiger was considered vulnerable to Soviet 45 mm guns firing subcaliber AP shot. The ranges given in the memo are similar to those obtained in Soviet tests.[140] The shorter model 1937 gun could penetrate the side and rear from up to 200 meters. No mention is made of the ability to penetrate the lower side armor from 350 meters. On the other hand, the longer model 1942 gun is credited with being able to take down a Tiger tank from 500 meters, while this could only be achieved by hitting the 62 mm thick lower side armor at that range.[141]

---

[139] *Anlage zu H.Dv. 469/3b Panzer-Beschußtafel 8,8 cm KwK 36 as published on February 15th, 1943*
[140] TsAMO RF F.38 Op.11377 D.12 L.8-12
[141] TsAMO RF F.500 Op.12480 D.137 L.587

According to the memo, the 57 mm ZIS-2 gun is capable of penetrating the front of a Tiger from 500 meters with subcaliber ammunition. The sides are vulnerable at a range of 600 meters.[142] In Soviet trials subcaliber shot was not used at all. The gun never fired at the sides at such a close range and was found to be able to penetrate the side from 1000 meters.[143]

Data for the 76 mm 3-K AA gun also differs. According to the memo, the gun was capable of penetrating the side of a Tiger at 500 meters (attained in the Soviet trials[144]), but also the front of the tank from 700 meters with subcaliber shot.[145] Subcaliber shot was not used with this gun in the trials held in April of 1943 and the author is not aware of any such ammunition being fielded for 76 mm AA guns.

The 76 mm F-34 was said to be capable of penetrating the front of the Tiger from 100 meters and the side from 700 meters with subcaliber AP shot.[146] While this was not done in Soviet trials held in April of 1943, it is quite likely that the Germans would have run into this new type of ammunition on the battlefield. This aligns with penetration values of the subcaliber shot given by Soviet tables.[147] The memo also mentions that massed fire can damage the tank and reduce its effectiveness or even disable it even if it does not penetrate the armor. The Tiger is also said to be vulnerable to the T-34's gun from 500 meters in the front and 1500 m in the sides, although the type of ammunition is not specified.[148]

Like the 57 mm ZIS-2 gun, the performance of the 85 mm 52-K AA gun was also underestimated. It is given as being able to penetrate the sides from 1000 meters and unable to penetrate the front at all,[149] despite penetration of the

---

[142] TsAMO RF F.500 Op.12480 D.137 L.587
[143] TsAMO RF F.38 Op.11377 D.12 L.14-17
[144] TsAMO RF F.38 Op.11377 D.12 L.30
[145] TsAMO RF F.500 Op.12480 D.137 L.587
[146] TsAMO RF F.500 Op.12480 D.137 L.587
[147] TsAMO RF F.1233 Op.1 D.152 L.52
[148] TsAMO RF F.500 Op.12480 D.137 L.588
[149] TsAMO RF F.500 Op.12480 D.137 L.588

sides from 1450 meters and front from 1000 meters at 30 degrees in Soviet trials.[150]

Performance of heavier guns is also given in the German memo. The 122 mm A-19 gun penetrates the front of a Tiger from 1000 meters and the sides from 1500 meters.[151] While performance against the side armor can be extrapolated from the accidental penetration of the rear armor of the same thickness from 1500 meters, the catastrophic damage dealt to the Tiger's turret by a shot from the same range suggests that the front armor would be vulnerable at a range much greater than 1000 meters.[152] The much thicker front armor of the Ferdinand tank destroyer would be penetrated at a range of 1400 meters in later trials.[153]

Data for the 152 mm ML-20 gun-howitzer is also given, even though no data about the penetration of this gun was recorded in the trials held in April of 1943.[154] According to the German source, it was capable of penetrating the front of the Tiger from 500 meters and the side and rear from 1000 meters.[155] This is also likely a considerable underestimation of the ML-20's abilities. In aforementioned trials against the Ferdinand, the ML-20's armor piercing shell shattered the front armor composed of two 100 mm plates sandwiched together from a range of 1200 meters.[156]

The memo also notes that the Tiger is not invulnerable to mines. While damage dealt to the Tiger by anti-tank mines was slight, even minor damage is difficult to repair under combat circumstances. Furthermore, a disabled Tiger is difficult to recover due to its size and weight. If it is necessary to go through

---

[150] TsAMO RF F.38 Op.11377 D.12 L.33-36
[151] TsAMO RF F.500 Op.12480 D.137 L.587
[152] TsAMO RF F.38 Op.11377 D.12 L.37-38
[153] Y. Bakhurin, *Panzerjager Tiger (P) Ferdinand*, Tactical Press, Moscow, 2014, p.70
[154] TsAMO RF F.38 Op.11377 D.12 L.1
[155] TsAMO RF F.500 Op.12480 D.137 L.587
[156] Y. Bakhurin, *Panzerjager Tiger (P) Ferdinand*, Tactical Press, Moscow, 2014, p.71

minefields, Tigers must wait for engineers to make a passage. [157] It is likely that this advice was written as a result of the Battle of Kursk, where Tigers of the *schwere Panzer-Abteilung* 505 suffered considerable damage in minefields despite support from engineering units.[158]

Even though the performance of many of the Soviet weapons was underestimated, the memo reminds German commanders that their tanks were not invulnerable: "The frequently displayed opinion about the invulnerability of the PzKpfw VI is a mistake, and often leads to improper use of the Tiger tank, which causes excessive losses." The memo highlights the importance of thorough reconnaissance, especially when difficult terrain such as water hazards, bridges, and swamps are encountered. Tigers tanks must be used en masse and in cooperation with infantry. Lone Tiger tanks are quickly discovered and destroyed by Soviet artillery.[159]

The memo published in October of 1943 was based on only a limited amount of experience. Even though the Tiger was in service on the Soviet-German front for over a year at this point, the Battle of Kursk was its only major engagement. Many Soviet weapons designed to fight this tank had not yet reached the battlefield. While the memo already shows notes of concern about Soviet anti-tank weapons, the new Soviet heavy tank had not yet arrived on the scene. The appearance of the IS-2 made an impact on German tank crews and it was covered in a separate article published in the *Nachrichtenblatt der Panzertruppen* in September of 1944.[160]

The article stated in no uncertain terms that "Stalin tanks should not be engaged under any circumstances by Tigers in less than platoon strength (4 Tigers). To use single Tigers is to invite their destruction." and that "The legend

---

[157] TsAMO RF F.500 Op.12480 D.137 L.589. It is worth noting that the Russian language translation provided on page 787 of the document is incorrect and omits the double negative. Thanks to Bernhard Kast for noting this.

[158] C.W. Wilbeck, *Sledgehammers Strengths and Flaws of Tiger Tank Battalions in World War II*, The Aberjona Press, Bedford, 2004, pp.72-73

[159] TsAMO RF F.500 Op.12480 D.137 L.586

[160] Canadian Military Headquarters, London (CMHQ), Files Block No. 55 - 5777 Image 2098

of the 'thick hide', the 'invulnerability' and the 'safety' of the Tiger, which has sprung up in other arms of the service, as well as within the tank arm, must now be destroyed and dissipated."[161] Tiger crews were recommended to fire at the side and rear of "Stalin tanks", although one Tiger unit reported that the IS-2 could be penetrated frontally at ranges of under 500 meters. However, the article also notes that the IS-2 opens fire at over 2000 meters, at which range it can still destroy the Tiger.[162] This is consistent with Soviet instructions to deploy IS-2 tanks behind an echelon of medium tanks and engage the enemy at a range of 1500 to 2000 meters.[163]

Tiger Tactics

In addition to testing Tiger tanks on proving grounds, Soviet troops had a chance to observe the Tiger in its "natural habitat" at the Battle of Kursk. Red Army commanders were expecting this new type of tank, even though most of them had never seen it in real life. Warnings with photographs attached were distributed among front line troops.[164] Commanders were instructed to inform all troops in artillery and armored branches as well as anti-tank riflemen of this new tank, study its characteristics, and know how to fight it. This new threat was taken seriously, to the point where commanders were instructed to test their troops on their knowledge and report how well they knew the Tiger tank.[165] Study began as early as May 8th, 1943, just over a week after penetration trials were completed.[166]

Soviet officers carefully observed Tiger tanks on the battlefield. Knowing how the enemy used their newest weapon was key to defeating it. Information gathered by individual units was shared both upwards and laterally in order to

---

[161] Canadian Military Headquarters, London (CMHQ), Files Block No. 55 - 5777 Image 2099
[162] Canadian Military Headquarters, London (CMHQ), Files Block No. 55 - 5777 Image 2098
[163] TsAMO RF F.307 Op.4148 D.189 L.107
[164] TsAMO RF F.1739 Op.1 D.70 L.443
[165] TsAMO RF F.3335 Op.1 D.9 L.213-216
[166] TsAMO RF F.1140 Op.1 D.27 L.65

quickly form a full picture of the tactics used by Tiger tank units.[167] The first such messages were shared as early as July 10th, less than a week into the Battle of Kursk.[168]

According to POW interrogations, Tiger tanks were deployed in special battalions composed of four companies with 10-12 tanks each. Information obtained earlier that there were Tiger tanks in every tank division turned out to be false.[169] Tigers never fought alone, but in close cooperation with engineers, infantry, artillery, aircraft, assault guns, and other tank units.[170]

It was noted that considerable losses taken by Tiger units forced the Germans to become very careful in how Tigers were deployed.[171] Small groups of Tigers were deployed on the flanks of light or medium tank units. Spearheads of an assault were only made up of Tigers if a large number of these tanks was available. In either case, Tigers were accompanied by light or medium tanks.[172] Tigers were also very careful to stay with their infantry, never breaking away further than 150-200 meters from it.[173] Tigers drove at a speed of 5-6 kph so infantry could keep up, stopping to fire.[174] Tiger tanks also carried a reserve of tank riders, which could be deployed against any anti-tank guns that were spotted.[175]

Tiger tanks were extra careful when attacking along roads, sometimes advancing under the cover of smoke. Tiger tank attacks were supported by assault guns firing from hills at a range of 1-1.5 km.[176] One assault gun was issued for every three Tiger tanks.[177] AA guns were used to cover Tiger tanks

---

[167] TsAMO RF F.3384 Op1. D.13 L.18
[168] TsAMO RF F.3384 Op1. D.13 L.18
[169] TsAMO RF F.6231 Op.26929s D.2 L.26
[170] TsAMO RF F.442 Op.8465 D.64 L.30
[171] TsAMO RF F.3384 Op1. D.13 L.18
[172] TsAMO RF F.9623 Op.1 D.27 L.60
[173] TsAMO RF F.6231 Op.26929s D.2 L.26
[174] TsAMO RF F.9623 Op.1 D.27 L.60
[175] TsAMO RF F.6231 Op.26929s D.2 L.26
[176] TsAMO RF F.9623 Op.1 D.27 L.60
[177] TsAMO RF F.442 Op.8465 D.64 L.30

from air attack. When encountering strong anti-tank defenses, the Tigers aimed to bypass them rather than break through.[178]

Tiger crews were well aware of the thick armor of their tanks. Tiger tanks fighting in the first echelon of an attack would intentionally expose themselves, hoping to draw fire from impatient or inexperienced anti-tank gunners. If anti-tank guns revealed their positions, they would be attacked by infantry that accompanied the Tigers.[179]

As Tiger units sustained losses, the Germans began to use Tigers from ambushes, striking at the flanks of Soviet counterattacks. The tank's ability to fire at long range was heavily relied upon to keep them safe.[180]

Further observation and study of Tiger tanks on the battlefield was recommended.[181]

Next page: "Clover leaf" diagram published in the *Tigerfibel* showing the ranges at which a Tiger tank is guaranteed to destroy a T-34 (black) and the areas from which a T-34 can destroy a Tiger (gray). While the Soviet tank could be safely dispatched from a long range, the Tiger was by no means invulnerable, and an overconfident Tiger commander stood the risk of losing his tank.

---

[178] TsAMO RF F.9623 Op.1 D.27 L.60
[179] TsAMO RF F.442 Op.8465 D.64 L.30
[180] TsAMO RF F.3384 Op1. D.13 L.18
[181] TsAMO RF F.9623 Op.1 D.27 L.61

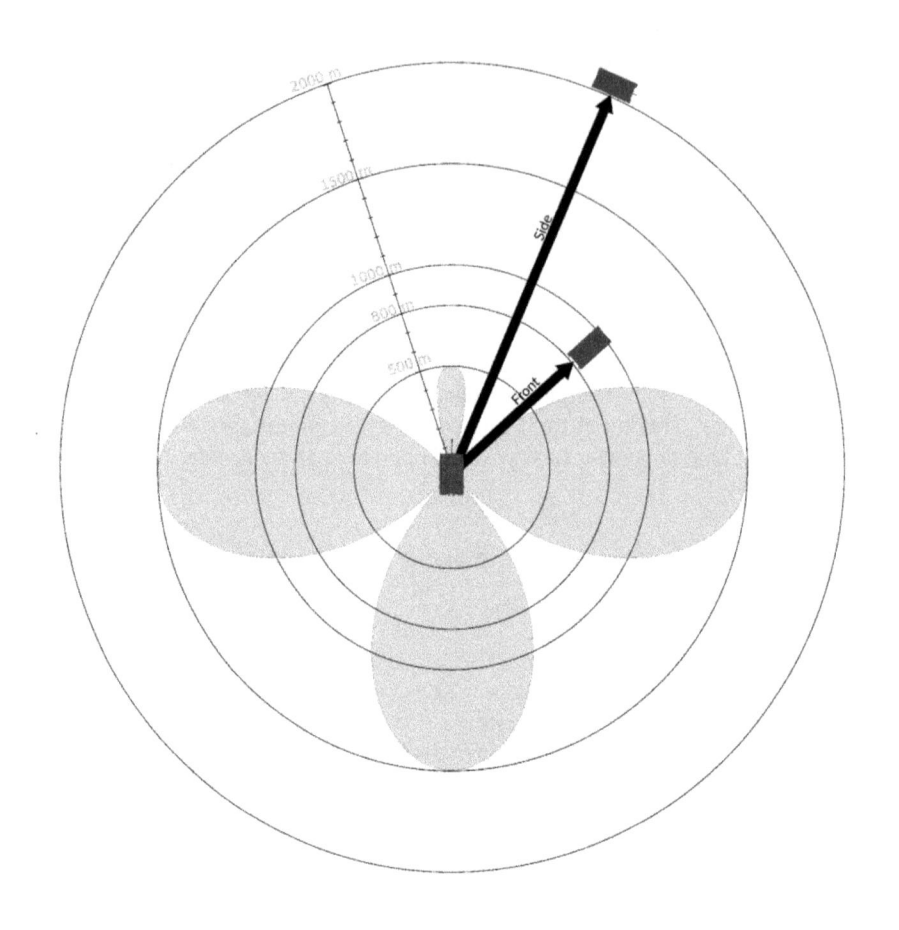

How to Kill a Tiger Tank

The primary purpose of studying these new tanks on the battlefield was to determine how to destroy them. Proving grounds trials formed a good basis for deciding which weapons were effective against the Tiger tank, but their performance in real life conditions was also carefully tracked.

The 76 mm ZIS-3 gun was found to be able to penetrate the front of the Tiger with subcaliber AP shot. Various sources gave the maximum range at which the front could be penetrated as high as 800 meters[182] although success was not guaranteed at this range.[183]

Ordinary 76 mm AP shells could penetrate the sides of the tank from ranges of up to 800 meters[184] or destroy its running gear.[185] The AP shell was ineffective against the tank's front armor, but several consecutive hits with AP shells could still result in penetration.[186] There were cases where Tiger tanks came under fire from 76 mm gun batteries and were not penetrated, but still retreated.[187] 76 mm HE was also listed as a method of knocking out Tigers, although no specifics were given. Given that the range in some examples was listed as high as 5700-5800 meters, it is likely that the shells struck the roof of the tank.[188] HE shells fired from 122 mm M-30 howitzers also proved effective at ranges of up to 1000 meters. Successful hits shattered weld seams, displaced the turret from the turret ring, and killed the crew.[189]

45 mm subcaliber shot could penetrate the side armor at close range and AP shells could destroy the running gear to immobilize the tank.[190] The 45 mm gun was effective at ranges of up to 500-600 meters.[191] This was consistent with

---

[182] TsAMO RF F.3384 Op1. D.13 L.18
[183] TsAMO RF F.9623 Op.1 D.27 L.60
[184] TsAMO RF F.9623 Op.1 D.27 L.60
[185] TsAMO RF F.3384 Op1. D.13 L.18
[186] TsAMO RF F.341 Op.5328 D.149 L.156
[187] TsAMO RF F.341 Op.5328 D.149 L.155
[188] TsAMO RF F.341 Op.5328 D.149 L.158
[189] TsAMO RF F.341 Op.5328 D.149 L.156
[190] TsAMO RF F.3384 Op1. D.13 L.18
[191] TsAMO RF F.9623 Op.1 D.27 L.60

data obtained during proving grounds trials. One issue with the use of 45 mm subcaliber shot was that the beyond armor effects were limited as a result of the small armor penetrating core, only 20 mm in diameter. This meant that a tank that was knocked out could be recovered and repaired relatively easily. Instructions were issued to tell the crews to ensure that tanks that were not just knocked out, but rendered unusable.[192] It was recommended to mix 45 and 76 mm guns when building anti-tank defenses. 45 mm guns could be used to fire at the light and medium tanks used in support of Tigers, while the more effective 76 mm guns could be used to fire at Tigers tanks.[193]

76 mm ZIS-3 divisional gun, Victory Park. This gun was nominally an all-purpose gun attached to infantry divisions, but these guns were also used in anti-tank artillery units. (Pavel Borovikov)

---

[192] TsAMO RF F.3475 Op.1 D.58 L.427
No details about the writer's definition of unusable are provided.
[193] TsAMO RF F.6231 Op.26929s D.2 L.27

Left side of the Tiger tank at Patriot Park, showing a vision slit and a pistol port in the turret. Firing at these weak spots might not destroy the tank, but it could reduce the crew's vision or harm them with splash. *(Pavel Borovikov)*

Infantry also had measures they could take against the Tiger. Anti-tank rifles might not have been able to penetrate the tank's main armor, but they could still knock out observation devices and vision slits.[194] Only one instance was mentioned where an anti-tank rifleman set a Tiger on fire by shooting it in the rear at close range.[195] Anti-tank grenades proved effective against the tank's running gear. Striking the vision slits, turret ring, or engine deck with a Molotov cocktail was another effective strategy.[196] Even without anti-tank weapons, infantry could still be useful when fighting Tigers in order to counter enemy infantry that sought out and destroyed anti-tank guns.[197]

---

[194] TsAMO RF F.3384 Op1. D.13 L.18
[195] TsAMO RF F.9623 Op.1 D.27 L.60
[196] TsAMO RF F.3384 Op1. D.13 L.18
[197] TsAMO RF F.6231 Op.26929s D.2 L.27

The reports concluded that the Tiger is vulnerable to all weapons previously used against German tanks.[198] It was noted that Tigers burn easily at the first penetration.[199] The large size of the tank and its slow speed made it a good target for anti-tank gunners.[200] Even though some success was had knocking out Tigers at a range of up to 800 meters, some instructions suggested using 76 mm and smaller guns from ambushes at a range of 500 meters or less. It was also noted that the 85 mm AA gun could penetrate the side of a Tiger from 1450 meters and the front from 1000 meters.[201] A special note was made to only open fire at a range where your weapon was effective in order to avoid revealing your position to the enemy.[202]

It was suggested that in case of a tank attack, Tigers should be destroyed first, particularly since light and medium tanks would not continue the attack if the Tigers supporting them were knocked out.[203] Special mobile groups should be prepared whose only job was to fight Tiger tanks.[204] Special batteries should also be allocated to suppress the assault guns covering the Tigers.[205]

An illustrated manual on fighting Tiger tanks was composed based on the above information. The manual began with a reassurance that the new German tank was far from invincible. All weapons previously used against enemy tanks remained effective if used correctly.[206]

The first section of the manual focused on the tracks and running gear. The Tiger could be stopped by destroying the drive sprocket, idler, or track with any anti-tank gun, anti-tank grenade, or a mine. The manual suggested tying 3-4

---

[198] TsAMO RF F.3384 Op1. D.13 L.18
[199] Unfortunately, no explanation for this tendency to catch fire is provided.
[200] TsAMO RF F.6231 Op.26929s D.2 L.26
[201] TsAMO RF F.442 Op.8465 D.64 L.29
[202] TsAMO RF F.442 Op.8465 D.64 L.31
[203] TsAMO RF F.9623 Op.1 D.27 L.60
[204] TsAMO RF F.442 Op.8465 D.64 L.31
[205] TsAMO RF F.9623 Op.1 D.27 L.61
[206] Directorate of Armored and Mechanized Forces of the Red Army, *Naibolee uyazvimiye i porazhayemiye mesta nemetskogo tanka T-VI i sposoby borby s nim*, Military Publisher of the People's Commissariat of Defense of the USSR, Moscow, 1943, p.1

anti-tank mines to a board and then pulling the mines underneath an approaching tank with a rope.[207]

Side of the Tiger tank at Patriot Park. The vertical armor behind the wheels was only 62 mm thick, making it easier to penetrate than the 82 mm thick upper side. Unfortunately, it was difficult to hit this part of the tank as the interleaved road wheels acted as spaced armor. Note that the outermost wheel on this vehicle is missing. *(Pavel Borovikov)*

The next target described in the manual was the side of the tank. As discovered in the trials, the manual indicated that the lower side partially covered by road wheels was more vulnerable. However, the fuel and ammunition were stored behind the upper side armor. Successful penetration in this area with a 45, 57, or 76 mm gun could ignite or explode the tank. The same could be achieved by shooting the tank in the rear.[208] Another tempting target

---

[207] Directorate of Armored and Mechanized Forces of the Red Army, *Naibolee uyazvimiye i porazhayemiye mesta nemetskogo tanka T-VI i sposoby borby s nim*, Military Publisher of the People's Commissariat of Defense of the USSR, Moscow, 1943, p.2

[208] Directorate of Armored and Mechanized Forces of the Red Army, *Naibolee uyazvimiye i porazhayemiye mesta nemetskogo tanka T-VI i sposoby borby s nim*, Military Publisher of the People's Commissariat of Defense of the USSR, Moscow, 1943, p.3

for gunners was the 10 mm wide gap between the turret and hull roof. Landing a shell or even bullet there could jam the turret.[209]

Gun mantlet of the Tiger tank at Patriot Park. The Tiger's gun mantlet was an imposing target, but it had its weaknesses. Fire at the machine gun port, gun sight, or the gun could result in a mission kill. *(Pavel Borovikov)*

Riflemen were instructed to focus their fire on pistol ports and vision slits in the turret, vision slits in the commander's cupola, the driver's vision slit, and the periscopes on the front of the hull. Fire against these targets would blind the tank and could even injure the crew. The commander's cupola was also a tempting target for artillerymen, as a hit with any type of weapon would likely harm the commander. Even partial damage to the cupola would make it

---

[209] Directorate of Armored and Mechanized Forces of the Red Army, *Naibolee uyazvimiye i porazhayemiye mesta nemetskogo tanka T-VI i sposoby borby s nim*, Military Publisher of the People's Commissariat of Defense of the USSR, Moscow, 1943, p.5

vulnerable to close range attack with grenades or Molotov cocktails.[210] Molotov cocktails could also be thrown at the engine deck and at the roof above the driver's compartment.[211]

Hull machine gun mount of the Tiger tank at Patriot Park. A hit here could penetrate the armor even if it otherwise would not have, killing the hull gunner/radio operator. *(Pavel Borovikov)*

Fire against the tank's cannon and machine gun is also effective. Damaging the gun or jamming the gun mount with any type of weapon would result in a

---

[210] Directorate of Armored and Mechanized Forces of the Red Army, *Naibolee uyazvimiye i porazhayemiye mesta nemetskogo tanka T-VI i sposoby borby s nim*, Military Publisher of the People's Commissariat of Defense of the USSR, Moscow, 1943, pp.3-4.

[211] Directorate of Armored and Mechanized Forces of the Red Army, *Naibolee uyazvimiye i porazhayemiye mesta nemetskogo tanka T-VI i sposoby borby s nim*, Military Publisher of the People's Commissariat of Defense of the USSR, Moscow, 1943, p.5

mission kill and penetrating the hull machine gun with an anti-tank rifle would also kill the radio operator/hull gunner or disable the machine gun.[212]

Anti-Tiger Ammunition

No time was wasted developing improved ammunition for use against Tiger tanks. Subcaliber AP shot for 57, and 76 mm guns[213] as well as HEAT for 122 mm guns[214] became available in June of 1943. A memo describing the effectiveness of these new weapons was written by the GAU (*Glavnoye Artilleriyskoye Upravleniye*, Main Artillery Directorate) and circulated among the artillery commanders of Fronts and Armies.[215]

45 mm subcaliber shot was described as an effective weapon against the sides of a Tiger tank at ranges of up to 300 meters.[216] This was a known quantity, as 45 mm subcaliber AP shot was already tested against the Tiger in April of 1943.[217]

57 mm subcaliber shot was a much more effective weapon, penetrating up to 175 mm of armor at normal at a range of 100 meters. At 1000 meters the penetration dropped to 95 mm. It was forbidden to use this shot when firing at targets at a range of over 1000 meters.[218] 76 mm subcaliber AP shot was somewhat less potent, with a maximum penetration of only 132 mm at 90 degrees, dropping to 96 mm at 500 meters. Using this ammunition at ranges of over 500 meters was forbidden.[219] It is no accident that it was forbidden to use this ammunition at ranges where penetration fell below 100 mm, as the Tiger

---

[212] Directorate of Armored and Mechanized Forces of the Red Army, *Naibolee uyazvimiye i porazhayemiye mesta nemetskogo tanka T-VI i sposoby borby s nim*, Military Publisher of the People's Commissariat of Defense of the USSR, Moscow, 1943, p.4
[213] TsAMO RF F.3481 Op.1 D.140 L.262
[214] TsAMO RF F.9604 Op.1 D.38 L.229
[215] TsAMO RF F.983 Op.1 D.26 L.20
[216] TsAMO RF F.983 Op.1 D.26 L.20
[217] TsAMO RF F.38 Op.11377 D.12 L.8-9
[218] TsAMO RF F.3481 Op.1 D.140 L.262
[219] TsAMO RF F.3481 Op.1 D.140 L.263

was explicitly named as their intended target. Using this special shot against lightly armored tanks while ordinary AP shells were available was also forbidden.[220]

For weapons with a lower muzzle velocity such as the 122 mm M-30 howitzer, the preferred ammunition to use against heavy tanks was HEAT. The BP-460A shell penetrated up to 100 mm of armor and was considered an effective means of fighting enemy tanks at ranges of up to 1000 meters. Due to a low muzzle velocity, hitting even a Tiger-sized target at a greater range was unlikely.[221] 76 mm HEAT was also developed, but this type of shell insufficiently powerful to combat a Tiger tank.[222]

The 152 mm ML-20 gun-howitzer was a special case. Rather than a HEAT shell or subcaliber AP shot, it received an AP shell.[223] Concrete piercing shells used in pre-war trials penetrated 90 mm of armor at point-blank range,[224] but this new and improved AP shell was considered to be an effective weapon against even the Tiger's front armor at a range of up to 1000 meters.[225] This was a very conservative estimate, since in live fire trials against a Ferdinand tank destroyer held in December of 1943 the ML-20's armor piercing shell shattered the front armor composed of two 100 mm plates sandwiched together from a range of 1200 meters.[226]

---

[220] TsAMO RF F.3481 Op.1 D.140 L.263
[221] TsAMO RF F.3481 Op.1 D.140 L.263-264
[222] TsAMO RF F.983 Op.1 D.26 L.21
[223] TsAMO RF F.983 Op.1 D.26 L.21
[224] TsAMO RF F.81 Op.12104 D.261 L.8
[225] TsAMO RF F.983 Op.1 D.26 L.21
[226] Y. Bakhurin, *Panzerjager Tiger (P) Ferdinand*, Tactical Press, Moscow, 2014, p.71

Further Trials and Research

Even though official penetration trials and observation of Tiger tanks at the Battle of Kursk gave a pretty good overview of the degree of the Tiger's protection, field penetration trials were still carried out by individual units.

The first field trials were carried out against a freshly captured Tiger tank at the Battle of Kursk, on July 21st, 1943, by the 9th Tank Corps. 37 and 85 mm AA guns as well as 45 and 76 mm tank guns were used in these trials. The results were similar to those obtained in official trials three months earlier. The 37 mm gun could not penetrate the Tiger's armor at all. This weapon could only destroy the tracks and wheels at a range of 300-400 meters. 45 mm subcaliber AP penetrated the side of the tank's hull and turret at 200 meters. The AP shell was ineffective. Similarly, 76 mm AP shells proved ineffective and only subcaliber AP shot could penetrate the side of the tank from 400 meters. The 85 mm AA gun could penetrate the side of the tank from 1200 meters. The report recommended stopping the tank first by destroying its running gear and then destroying it with concentrated fire against the sides.[227] Interestingly enough, these trials were later called out by the Chief of Staff of Artillery of the Red Army Lieutenant-General Samsonov[228] as not representative. According to Samsonov, other trials proved that the range at which the Tiger could be penetrated with these weapons was significantly greater than reported by the 9th Tank Corps.[229]

The 160th Independent Tank Destroyer Battalion also tested their 45 mm guns against a Tiger tank on January 18th, 1944. The results were, as expected, discouraging. At a range of 600 meters, AP-incendiary shells (with the same ballistics as ordinary AP shells, but carrying an incendiary charge) fired by the 45 mm gun simply disintegrated upon hitting the Tiger's front armor. 45 mm subcaliber AP shot ricocheted, causing no effect. The effect against the tank's running gear was good and a 45 mm gun could still immobilize a Tiger tank.[230]

---

[227] TsAMO RF F.3408 Op.1 D.30 L.74-76
[228] No relation to the author.
[229] TsAMO RF F.959 Op.1 D.355 L.16
[230] TsAMO RF F.1410 Op.1 D.220 L.113

Running gear of the Tiger tank at Patriot Park. The width of the Tiger's track meant that it was difficult to destroy with solid shot or even an AP shell with a small bursting charge. *(Pavel Borovikov)*

A similar trial was carried out by the 3rd Belorussian Front on November 13th-14th, 1944. 45 mm anti-tank guns, 14.5 mm anti-tank rifles, and anti-tank hand grenades were used. This trial specifically focused on immobilizing the tank by attacking its drive sprocket and tracks.[231]

---

[231] TsAMO RF F.10895 Op.1 D.7 L.146

It was found that an AP shell or subcaliber AP shot that hit the center of a track link from 200-300 meters only made a hole in the track link. However, if the shell hit a track pin, it shattered the pin and both the links attached to it. The best way to fire at the track was not head on, but at a 45 degree angle, since the hole made in the tracks was larger as a result and several links could be destroyed in one shot. Two hits were scored on the drive sprocket during the trials, which destroyed it completely.

Just like the 45 mm gun, the 14.5 mm anti-tank rifle could penetrate the tracks, but to a much lesser effect. 14.5 mm bullets only made a small hole in the track links and 4-5 hits to the same link were needed in order to sever the track. Anti-tank rifle fire against Tiger tracks was deemed ineffective.

Anti-tank grenades (likely the RPG-40 filled with 760 grams of TNT) were thrown under the tracks from a distance of 10 meters. A single grenade under the tracks destroyed half of the track, immobilizing the tank. A bundle of two grenades destroyed the track completely. Grenades detonated under the tank also had an effect. One grenade would bend the floor and a bundle of two grenades would break through it.[232]

Penetration trials were also conducted by the 2nd battalion of the 63rd Guards Tank Brigade on June 16th, 1944. 76 mm F-34 (curiously, the report says ZIS-5 even though the brigade only had T-34 tanks and no KVs) and 85 mm ZIS-S-53 guns were used in these trials. The 76 mm gun fired first with AP shells, aiming at the side of the tank from 600 meters. No penetrations were achieved despite 16 hits. 10 shots were fired at a range of 400 meters, two of which penetrated the lower side armor and two penetrated the upper side. The tank then closed in to 300 meters, firing subcaliber AP shot at the turret. One hit was scored on the turret ring, jamming it. The second hit the gun mantlet, disabling the gun.[233] The trials report noted that even in cases where 76 mm shells left only dents, enough spalling was caused on the opposite side of the armor plate to kill the Tiger's crew.[234]

---

[232] TsAMO RF F.10895 Op.1 D.7 L.146
[233] TsAMO RF F.3161 Op.1 D.11 L.66
[234] TsAMO RF F.3161 Op.1 D.11 L.67

The trials then switched to an 85 mm gun. The 85 mm gun fired at the front of the tank from 600 meters. One shot ricocheted, but four penetrated the front armor and knocked out the driver's observation device. All shells that penetrated burst within the tank. Four more shots were made at a range of 1300 meters, but none penetrated.[235]

Driver's observation device of the Tiger tank at Patriot Park. The device was protected with a thick shutter, but it was still a weak point. Even shells that otherwise wouldn't penetrate could be aimed here to blind the driver by destroying his vision block or jamming the shutter shut. *(Pavel Borovikov)*

The 85 mm gun also fired at the side of the Tiger under test. Two shots penetrated the side from 800 meters. From 1300 meters, one shot penetrated the side armor and another left a dent. As with the 76 mm gun, nonpenetrating hits resulted in spalling that could kill the crew.[236]

---

[235] TsAMO RF F.3161 Op.1 D.11 L.66-67
[236] TsAMO RF F.3161 Op.1 D.11 L.67

Performance of the 122 mm M-30 howitzer against Tiger tanks in combat was carefully recorded by the 305th Howitzer Artillery Regiment of the Supreme Command Reserve during battles around Gorodisk (presumably Grodzisk, Poland) in August of 1944. In particular, the performance of 122 mm HEAT shells was analyzed. 122 mm HEAT penetrated a 100 mm thick plate 10 out of 10 times in trials when placed at normal and 7 out of 10 times when placed at a 30 degree angle, making it an effective weapon against the Tiger tank.[237]

The howitzer batteries found that these shells were indeed effective. They reported that the front armor of a Tiger could be penetrated at a range of 500 meters (see discussion on HEAT and range below) with 400-600 meters as the optimal range to open fire. The side was vulnerable at a range of up to 800 meters, provided the angle of impact was close to normal. The tracks could be destroyed at 1200 meters, but firing HEAT at ranges of over 1000 meters was generally ineffective. In comparison, medium tanks were considered to be viable targets at ranges of up to 800-900 meters and lightly armored targets like APCs could be destroyed at any range.[238] The ranges given here are subject to some discussion. Nominally, the penetration value of a HEAT shell is not affected by its velocity, and therefore range to the target. However, the low muzzle velocity of howitzers significantly impacted the chance to hit. In the case of the 122 mm M-30 model 1938 howitzer, a HEAT shell fired using the 4th charge had a muzzle velocity of just 290 m/s. At a range of 1000 meters, the height of the shell's trajectory would be 10 meters, with the shell impacting its target at an angle of 3.75 degrees from horizontal. The time of flight would be 3.4 seconds, making it very difficult to hit a moving target.[239] A probable error of 0.6 m horizontally and vertically gave the weapon sufficient precision to hit a tank-sized target head on, but only if the range was properly estimated.[240] The gunnery tables for this gun gave 1000 meters as the most effective range, although sight settings for ranges up to 2000 meters were provided.[241]

---

[237] RGASPI F.644 Op.2 D.170 L.177
[238] TsAMO RF F.11243 Op.1 D.18 L.87
[239] *Tablitsy strelby 122-mm gaubitsy obr. 1938 g., 5th annotated edition*, Military Publisher of the People's Commissariat of Defense, Moscow, 1943, p.56-57
[240] *Tablitsy strelby 122-mm gaubitsy obr. 1938 g., 5th annotated edition*, Military Publisher of the People's Commissariat of Defense, Moscow, 1943, p.87
[241] *Tablitsy strelby 122-mm gaubitsy obr. 1938 g., 5th annotated edition*, Military Publisher of the People's Commissariat of Defense, Moscow, 1943, p.2

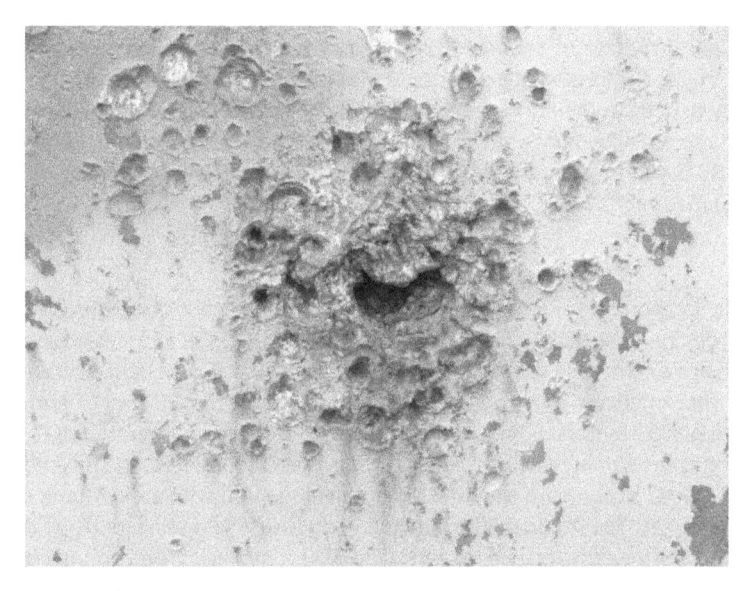

A hole in the Tiger's armor, Lenino-Snegiri. The blast of the explosive charge in a HEAT shell is concentrated, causing a small hole like this one but catastrophic damage on the inside. These shells were commonly used by low velocity guns, as the velocity of the shell does not play an effect on its penetration. *(Pavel Borovikov)*

Another trial was carried out by the 1st Howitzer Artillery Brigade of the Supreme Command Reserve in November of 1944. The Tiger tank was already old news since the Tiger II had been discovered, and indeed the majority of the trial focuses on penetration of Tiger II tanks. Nevertheless, a Tiger is still included in the mix. All shots were made from a range of 1000 meters.

The 100 mm BS-3 gun (field gun with ballistics identical to the D-10T mentioned above) fired first. One hit was scored on the side armor and one on the gun mantlet, both of which resulted in complete penetrations.[242]

The 122 mm D-25T gun installed in an IS-2 tank fired next. Three hits were scored on the front armor, each of which penetrated. The shells all burst inside

---

[242] TsAMO RF F.9755 Op.1 D.8 L.348

the tank. The trial report notes that hits from the 122 mm gun destroyed the Tiger tank completely to the point that it was no longer suitable to test the 152 mm gun-howitzer of the SU-152 SPG that was made available for trials that day.[243] Conclusions to the report state that both the BS-3 and D-25T guns can easily penetrate the armor of the Tiger at 1000 meters. The area allocated for trials did not allow firing at a longer range, but the report author estimated that the BS-3 gun remained effective against a Tiger tank out to a range of 1500-2000 meters.[244]

Old weapons were also re-tested in 1944. The arrival of first the GMC M10 tank destroyer and then the M4A2(76)W tank in the USSR and subsequent trials of their 76 mm guns gave the Red Army some food for thought. It turned out that the American 76 mm M62 shell penetrated up to 120 mm of armor at a range of 500 meters. Soviet shells of analogous caliber penetrated 100 mm of armor at the same velocity.[245] Special trials were conducted on December 28-30th, 1944, to compare the effect of the ammunition with a Tiger tank chosen as the target. The American 76 mm gun firing M62 shells at a muzzle velocity of 800 m/s showed excellent results. The 100 mm thick front armor could be penetrated from 1500 meters. The 82 mm thick side armor could be penetrated from 2000 meters. The Soviet 76 mm gun firing BR-350B shells at a muzzle velocity of 662 m/s did not perform as well. No attempt was made to penetrate the front armor of the Tiger. The 82 mm thick side armor could not be penetrated at a range of 100 meters, but could be penetrated at a range of 200 meters and even at 500 meters the odds of a penetration were 50%. This kind of unintuitive behavior was blamed on an incorrect setting of the fuse and orders were given to conduct additional trials.[246] Nevertheless, official trials confirmed the results of field trials: the 76 mm F-34 was not as helpless against the Tiger's side armor as trials held in 1943 would suggest.

---

[243] TsAMO RF F.9755 Op.1 D.8 L.349
[244] TsAMO RF F.9755 Op.1 D.8 L.350
[245] Y. Pasholok, *SU-76 amerikanskogo proizvodstva*, https://warspot.ru/8112-su-76-amerikanskogo-proizvodstva, retrieved on November 27th, 2023
[246] TsAMO RF F.38 Op.11369 D.709 L.3-4

Close-up of the Tiger's gun mantlet, Lenino-Snegiri. The dents and holes allow one to appreciate the protection offered by the Tiger's armor, but also show that it could be defeated. *(Pavel Borovikov)*

Experience with Tiger tanks was not limited to shooting them up on proving grounds, but also by driving them into battle. However, these cases were rare. For instance, the 9th Mechanized Corps reported capturing two intact Tiger tanks on August 30th, 1944. Both tanks broke down irreparably over the course of a 120-150 km march and had to be left behind.[247] The whole 3rd Guards Tank Army that the 9th Mechanized Corps belonged to reported that no cases of captured tanks being used in combat occurred in 1943-1944, in part due to a lack of trained crews and gasoline.[248]

The 51st Independent Motorcycle Regiment was the largest user of Tiger tanks within the Red Army, fielding five such vehicles in July of 1944. Despite going through refurbishment in Soviet factories, 1-2 were constantly undergoing repairs. 3 Tigers were still operational by August 19th, 1944, when

---

[247] TsAMO RF F.315 Op.4440 D.311 L.241
[248] TsAMO RF F.315 Op.4440 D.311 L.239

they were removed from the unit.[249] Tanks that were evacuated to Soviet repair factories could not always be put into fighting shape, in part due to a lack of gun sights. A proposal was made to use Soviet gun sights instead.[250] Another more radical proposal was made on November 28th, 1944. Instead of replacing the sight, the whole gun would be replaced. Designs were prepared for the installation of a 100 mm D-10T gun with a TSh-17 sight. As no changes were required to the gun mantlet, conversion only took 90 man-hours. Rather than using these vehicles as gun tanks, they would be dug in as fortifications. The project was approved, but never put into production.[251] This was not for lack of Tigers, as by June of 1945 the Red Army had 48 running Tigers, 36 more that needed repairs, and 8 tanks beyond repair in the 1-2 Belorussian Front, 1-3 Ukrainian Fronts, and the Courland group.[252]

Interestingly enough, the end of the war did not mean the end of trials. Metallurgical examinations of Panther and Tiger armor were performed in October of 1945 by scientists at NII-48. The results were quite interesting, especially when compared to German requirements for tank armor.[253]

German requirements for steel alloy used in 85-120 mm armor plates were as follows.

	C	Mn	Si	Cr	Ni	Mo	V	P	S
August 1942 to June 1944	0.32-0.42	0.30-0.65	0.15-0.50	2.00-2.40	-	0.20-0.30	-	up to 0.05	up to 0.05
After June 1944	0.37-0.47	0.60-0.90	0.20-0.50	1.60-1.90	-	-	up to 0.15	up to 0.05	up to 0.05

---

[249] Y. Pasholok, *Tyazheliy Trofey*, https://warspot.ru/9797-tyazhyolyy-trofey, retrieved on October 26th, 2023
[250] TsAMO RF F.81 Op.12038 D.385 L.69
[251] TsAMO RF F.81 Op.12038 D.775 L.8
[252] P. Samsonov, *Captured German Tanks in the Red Army*, https://www.tankarchives.ca/2016/07/captured-german-tanks-in-red-army.html, retrieved on December 15th, 2023
[253] A. Volgin, *Tolstaya shkura nemetskogo zverya*, https://warspot.ru/16322-tolstaya-shkura-nemetskogo-zverintsa, retrieved on November 4th, 2023

While the values observed in the captured tanks were:

	C	Mn	Si	Cr	Ni	Mo	V	P	S
Lower front plate 1, 100 mm	0.32	0.45	0.27	2.00	0.12	0.22	-	0.016-0.020	0.016-0.020
Lower front plate 2, 102 mm	0.33	0.78	0.28	2.61	1.73	-	-	-	-

The hardness of the two plates was 285-302 and 255-269 HBW respectively. This was somewhat harder than the 220-265 range specified for 85-120 mm thick steel. The Soviet report notes that the two plates taken from Tiger tanks had very different alloys and were hardened to different hardnesses, even though they were taken from the same component on two different tanks. This phenomenon was not exclusive to the Tiger. Among Panther and Tiger II tanks tested as a part of the same study, it was not uncommon to see wildly different chemical compositions and hardnesses of armor even on different plates of similar thickness and function on the same tank, let alone two different ones.[254]

The Soviet study concluded that this inconsistency was the result of the volatility of access to alloying elements in Germany. The lack of alloying elements reduced the quality of 100 mm thick armor and caused crystalline fractures in tests, which correlated to cracking and spalling under fire.[255]

The shortage of alloying elements negatively impacted the performance of armor in penetration trials. All plates shattered when subjected to fire from an 85 mm gun. 82 mm thick plates taken from the side of Tiger tanks that contained chrome but no nickel shattered on the first or second hit. Plates with both nickel and chrome stood up better, shattering on the third or fourth hit. Plates with less chrome and more nickel than the previously tested plates installed at a 30 degree angle showed cracks after 3-4 hits, but did not shatter. 100 mm thick plates also performed poorly. One plate shattered after a second hit and the second had so many cracks running through it after the first hit that further trials

---

[254] A. Volgin, *Tolstaya shkura nemetskogo zverya*, https://warspot.ru/16322-tolstaya-shkura-nemetskogo-zverintsa, retrieved on November 4th, 2023

[255] A. Volgin, *Tolstaya shkura nemetskogo zverya*, https://warspot.ru/16322-tolstaya-shkura-nemetskogo-zverintsa, retrieved on November 4th, 2023

were deemed pointless. The toughness of 82 and 100 mm thick plates was considered unsatisfactory by Soviet metallurgical standards.[256]

A Tiger tank on display at Lenino-Snegiri. Judging by the overall poor condition and many penetrations in its armor, this tank was subject to gunnery trials or served as a range target. *(Pavel Borovikov)*

---

[256] A. Volgin, *Tolstaya shkura nemetskogo zverya*, https://warspot.ru/16322-tolstaya-shkura-nemetskogo-zverintsa, retrieved on November 4th, 2023

Conclusions

In a way, the Soviet tank industry was ready for the Tiger. Work on 85 mm tank guns began back in 1940[257] and work on 120 mm thick armor that could withstand a hit from an 88 mm armor piercing shell began in 1941.[258] A chassis to combine all these elements in one tank was also already in development with the IS-1 in the spring of 1943.[259] A chassis for a tank destroyer with the same gun was also already available after the introduction of the SU-122.[260] Because of this, vehicles capable of fighting Tigers were put into service relatively quickly. More powerful guns such as the 100 mm D-10 and 122 mm D-25 put into development after encountering the Tiger proved useful to combat the Panther and Ferdinand. While even more powerful weapons were developed during the Great Patriotic War, they were never put into production.[261] The guns put into production after the Tiger's appearance turned out to be powerful enough to fight its successor, the Tiger II, as well.[262]

Trials of the Tiger had no effect on the T-43 medium tank in development at the time,[263] but the appearance of the Panther resulted in such radical alterations to the requirements for the tank that it was easier to scrap the project and start again with the T-44.[264] The up-armored T-34-85M tank tested in February of 1944 was also shot at not by the Tiger's 88 mm KwK 36 or 88 mm Flak 36, but by the newer 75 mm KwK 42 and 88 mm Pak 43 guns, showing that the latest threats overshadowed the Tiger's appearance earlier that year.[265]

---

[257] Y. Pasholok, *Sovetskiye Istrebiteli Tankov s Krugovym Obstrelom*, https://warspot.ru/4819-u-20-sovetskie-istrebiteli-tankov-s-krugovym-obstrelom, retrieved on October 30th, 2023

[258] Y. Pasholok, *KV-3: Nabor tankovoy massy*, https://warspot.ru/4960-kv-3-nabor-tankovoy-massy, retrieved on November 3rd, 2023

[259] RGASPI F.644 Op.2 D.138 L.194-195

[260] RGASPI F.644 Op.2 D.165 L.88

[261] TsAMO RF F.81 Op.12063 D.1 L.45

[262] TsAMO RF F.38 Op.11377 D.129 L.1-50

[263] Y. Pasholok, *Promezhutochnoye zveno*, https://warspot.ru/14603-promezhutochnoe-zveno, retrieved on November 5th, 2023

[264] Y. Pasholok, *Shag v nuzhnom napravlenii*, https://warspot.ru/14932-shag-v-nuzhnom-napravlenii, retrieved on November 5th, 2023

[265] Y. Pasholok, *Tupikovoye usileniye*, https://warspot.ru/15249-tupikovoe-usilenie, retrieved on November 5th, 2023

At the same time, it is not fair to say that the Tiger had been entirely forgotten. The publishing of a new manual on fighting Tiger tanks in June of 1944[266] and its continued presence in field trials[267] suggest that the infamous tank was still on the minds of front line troops even long after the more common Panther and more imposing Ferdinand made their debut. The fact that Soviet movie replicas built in the 1960s were patterned after Tigers suggests that it found its place in popular culture as the quintessential German tank.[268]

---

[266] TsAMO RF F.358 Op.5916 D.716 L.124-125
[267] TsAMO RF F.3161 Op.1 D.11 L.67
[268] N. Saichuk, *Tigry iz Lvova*, https://warspot.ru/21311-tigry-iz-lvova, retrieved on November 5th, 2023

The Anglo-American View
Debut in North Africa

Tiger tanks were deployed against the Western Allies not long after the first tanks of this type were sent to fight at Leningrad. Hitler had to take drastic measures to stop the successful offensive that began in North Africa following Rommel's defeat at El Alamein. This included deployment of the *schwere Panzer-Abteilung* 501 (501st Heavy Tank Battalion).[269] Tiger tanks issued to this battalion were specially prepared for employment in a tropical climate. The first three Tigers arrived in Bizerte, Tunisia, on November 23rd, 1942. Crews were brought in by aircraft.[270] The tanks went into battle soon after in small scale actions to defend approaches to the port they just disembarked at.[271] Tanks were attached to *Kampfgruppe* Lueder as they arrived, going into battle in small numbers starting on December 1st, 1942. 7 Tigers were operational on December 26th, 11 by December 31st, and by January 15th, 1943, the Germans were able to form three tank groups with a total of 13 Tigers.[272]

Meanwhile, the Tigers' opponents knew precious little about these tanks other than that they existed. The American Tactical and Technical Trends magazine contained just two short paragraphs on this tank, most of which contained educated guesses rather than facts. It was expected that the Mark VI, as the magazine referred to the Tiger, would be heavier than the Pz.Kpfw.III or Pz.Kpfw.IV, combining their best features into one tank. There was no data about the armament, but the author guessed that it would carry a weapon based on either the 7.5 cm Pak 40 anti-tank gun or 8.8 cm Flak. Face hardened armor as thick as 80 or 100 mm was expected with the use of spaced armor being likely. The article also mentioned a POW who reported that he belonged to an independent tank battalion during interrogation. In his words, the battalion was

---

[269] C.W. Wilbeck, *Sledgehammers Strengths and Flaws of Tiger Tank Battalions in World War II*, The Aberjona Press, Bedford, 2004, p.39

[270] W. Schneider, *Tigers in Combat I*, Stackpole Books, Mechanicsburg, 2004 p.41

[271] C.W. Wilbeck, *Sledgehammers Strengths and Flaws of Tiger Tank Battalions in World War II*, The Aberjona Press, Bedford, 2004, p.39

[272] W. Schneider, *Tigers in Combat I*, Stackpole Books, Mechanicsburg, 2004 p.42-43

armed with 50 ton tanks armed with 88 mm guns capable of a speed of 50 kph. It was not known whether or not this was actually the Mark VI.[273]

One source of information was a photograph published in the *National Zeitung* newspaper on December 11th, 1942. The photo showed the front portion of a Tiger tank with turret number 142 from the *schwere Panzer-Abteilung* 501 driving through Tunis. The muzzle brake was removed and transport tracks were installed.[274] Nevertheless, it allowed the Americans to work out the approximate dimensions of a Tiger and extrapolate its looks. The 20th edition of Tactical and Technical Trends published on March 11, 1943, included a drawing of the tank based on this photograph.[275]

Information from intelligence slowly trickled in. Gladeon Barnes, a key figure in American tank development and at the time Chief of the Technical Division of the Ordnance Department, received a description of the characteristics of two yet unnamed German tanks on February 23rd, 1943. Both tanks resembled the Pz.Kpfw.IV visually and had over 100 mm of front armor. The tanks carried powerful guns with a muzzle brake in fully rotating turrets, one 105 mm and the other 150 mm. Barnes forwarded the information on to Chief of Requirements Section, Army Ground Forces, Major General Richard C. Moore, indicating that while unconfirmed, this intelligence was sufficient warning to continue development of more powerful guns.[276]

It was not long before the Allies would have a lot more to go on than photographs and rumors. The first Tiger to be captured was knocked out on January 31st, 1943, but the Germans managed to demolish it before it fell into

---

[273] United States War Department, *Tactical and Technical Trends, No. 18*, Washington, 1943. p.6

[274] Getty Images, *2. World War, Northafrica, theater of war:German tank VI 'Tiger' in Tunis (Tunesia) - December 1942*, https://www.gettyimages.co.uk/detail/news-photo/world-war-northafrica-theater-of-war-german-tank-vi-tiger-news-photo/542370013, retrieved on November 6th, 2023

[275] United States War Department, *Tactical and Technical Trends, No. 20*, Washington, 1943. p.8

[276] NARA File No.GNRQT/34215

the hands of their enemy.[277] Nevertheless, the vehicle was a valuable source of information, as even a demolished and blown out husk could be measured to establish the armor protection of Germany's newest tank. Tactical and Technical Trends #20 published more than just a picture of the Tiger. Even though it was not yet conclusively established whether or not this was the Mark VI (now called Pz.Kw.6), hard data was available. The tank was said to weigh between 56 and 62 tons (potentially a unit conversion issue, as 62 Imperial tons is approximately equal to 56 metric tonnes, the correct weight of a Tiger tank). The thickness of the front armor was measured at 4 inches (102 mm), the sides of the hull and turret were 3.2 inches (82 mm) thick, and the floor and roof were 1 inch (26 mm) thick. The lower side armor behind the bogies was 2.4 inches (62 mm) thick. The thickness of the gun mantlet was estimated to be as much as 7.9 inches (200 mm). Unlike what was previously suspected, spaced armor was not used and the main armor was not face hardened.[278]

The tank was measured at 20 feet long, 12 feet wide, and 9.5 feet high. The report emphasized the length of the gun, which extended past the front of the hull by a whole 7 feet. The gun was identified as "fir[ing] the same fixed ammunition as the usual 88 mm AA/AT gun", suggesting that the 8.8 cm KwK 36 L/56's heritage was also known. The use of special 2 foot wide transport tracks was also reported. Tigers in battle used tracks 2 feet 4.5 inches wide. The article mentioned that while a tank with such armor and armament appeared formidable, it was not invulnerable. Deployment of such a large and heavy tank no doubt presented considerable logistical difficulties. It was also said that 6-pounder armor piercing shot could penetrate the side of the tank at a range of at least 500 yards. In one case, out of 20 shots fired at the side of the tank 5 penetrated, one going all the way through the turret and out the other side.[279]

Efforts to figure out what this tank could be fought with were long underway. A memo titled "Appreciation of Effect of Introduction of German PzKw 'X' or 'Tiger' Tank" was composed on February 18th, 1943, by Brigadier Burns, chairman of the Canadian AFV Users' Committee. Burns gave some more

---

[277] W. Schneider, *Tigers in Combat I*, Stackpole Books, Mechanicsburg, 2004 p.43

[278] United States War Department, *Tactical and Technical Trends*, No. 20, Washington, 1943. pp.7-9

[279] United States War Department, *Tactical and Technical Trends*, No. 20, Washington, 1943. p.9

information about the Tiger's armor. It was relatively soft (Brinell hardness of 290-320), but he assumed that the Germans would try to use armor of a higher hardness or introduce spaced armor later on in the tank's production. As it stood, it was estimated that a Tiger's side could be penetrated by a 6-pdr Mark V gun from 1000-1200 yards. The Sherman's 75 mm gun would only be effective from 500 yards. It was estimated that the new 76 mm tank gun that the Americans were working on would be effective at a range of up to 2000 yards. This was also the range at which the Sherman's frontal armor could be penetrated by the Tiger's 88 mm gun. As it was impractical to put enough armor on a Sherman to withstand a hit, it was desirable to arm new Sherman tanks with a 76 mm gun or at least a 6-pounder to allow them to engage this new tank.[280] The new 17-pounder was said to be more effective than the 6-pounder, but no figures were given.[281]

Burns also made note of the Tiger's limited mobility due to its weight, although in his opinion the deployment of a Tiger would not be that much more difficult than that of a Churchill. According to him, if the Germans were determined enough, they could get a Tiger anywhere it was needed.[282]

The British never managed to capture a Tiger tank from *schwere Panzer-Abteilung* 501. The unit was committed to Operation *Ochsenkopf* (Ox Head). *Kampfgruppe* Lang began an attack on Sidi Nsir as a part of this operation on February 26th, 1943. Despite an initial success against a British outpost, the Tigers did not make it far. Forced to operate along the main road due to hilly terrain and muddy conditions, the Tigers could not bypass British defenses at Hunt's Gap. After an attempt to negotiate a minefield covered by anti-tank guns, only 2 of the 14 Tiger tanks in the *Kampfgruppe* were operational. 7 out of the 14 were stuck in the minefield. The British took advantage of the German inability to recover the tanks, and infantry counterattacks allowed British sappers to approach the disabled vehicles and demolish them. The Germans lost seven valuable tanks, but as a result the British were unable to study an intact

---

[280] Canadian Military Headquarters, London (CMHQ), Files Block No. 55 - 5772, Image 4920
[281] Canadian Military Headquarters, London (CMHQ), Files Block No. 55 - 5772, Image 4921
[282] Canadian Military Headquarters, London (CMHQ), Files Block No. 55 - 5772, Image 4921

Tiger. Having no battle-ready Tigers left by March 1st, 1943, *schwere Panzer-Abteilung* 501 retreated.[283] Remaining Tigers were handed over to *schwere Panzer-Abteilung* 504.[284]

Tiger 131, Bovington Tank Museum. This was the first Tiger tank captured intact by British forces. Study of this vehicle revealed a lot about the new German tank and German tank industry in general. *(Peter Samsonov)*

It was *schwere Panzer-Abteilung* 504 that finally "donated" a Tiger worthy of study to the British. Like *schwere Panzer-Abteilung* 501, its tanks began arriving piecemeal starting on March 12th, 1943. It took more than a month for the battalion to gather, with the last Tiger of 1st company, *schwere Panzer-Abteilung* 504, arriving on April 16th, 1943. Together with the tanks received from *schwere Panzer-Abteilung* 501 this made for 21 tanks ready for battle. The tanks were deployed soon after in Operation *Fliederblüte* (Lilac Bloom) on April 19th,

---

[283] C.W. Wilbeck, *Sledgehammers Strengths and Flaws of Tiger Tank Battalions in World War II*, The Aberjona Press, Bedford, 2004, p.53-54.

[284] C.W. Wilbeck, *Sledgehammers Strengths and Flaws of Tiger Tank Battalions in World War II*, The Aberjona Press, Bedford, 2004, p.57

1943.[285] On April 24th the Tigers engaged the 2nd Sherwood Foresters supported by Churchill tanks of the 48th Royal Tank Regiment at Point 174, 10 miles northeast of Djebel Djaffa. Upon cresting the hill, a Tiger tank with turret number 131 came under fire from 6-pounder guns of Churchill III tanks at neighboring Point 151, a PIAT, and a captured 7.5 cm Pak 97/38 deployed by the 2nd Sherwood Foresters.[286] A 6-pounder shot struck the front of the tank, ricocheting down from the gun, jamming the turret of the tank, splitting the weld seam on the hull roof and damaging the radio. The radio operator and driver were likely wounded by this hit. The crew bailed out, abandoning their tank. It was recovered by the British several days later.[287]

Tiger 131, Bovington Tank Museum. Damage from the shot that struck the bottom of the gun mantlet underneath the gun and resulted in the loss of the tank can still be seen. *(Peter Samsonov)*

---

[285] W. Schneider, *Tigers in Combat I*, Stackpole Books, Mechanicsburg, 2004, pp.193-194

[286] D. Oscroft, *The Myth of Tiger 131*, https://tankmuseum.org/article/the_myth_of_tiger_131, retrieved on November 6th, 2023

[287] The Tank Museum, *Capture of Tiger 131*, https://tankmuseum.org/article/capture_of_tiger_131, retrieved on November 6th, 2023

In addition to Tiger 131, the British captured some POWs who could shine a light on the purpose of this new vehicle. According to interrogations, the Tiger's role was chiefly to accompany lighter units from the rear, providing cover for Pz.Kpfw.III and Pz.Kpfw.IV tanks. Once the medium tanks encountered resistance, they spread out and allowed the Tigers to engage. One POW indicated that Tigers would aim to engage enemy tanks from hull down positions at close range (as short as 250 yards or 229 m), although this does not match other testimony and observations. Tiger crews were aware of their gun's long range and fought at a distance, even to the point of acting as mobile artillery with forward observers correcting fire. [288]

This intelligence bulletin compared the information received from German POWs to experience in the USSR. The Soviets also wrote that the Tigers were being used to support medium tanks in battle when attacking or as mobile pillboxes when defending, hiding in ambushes for days. In this case, the tanks were deployed in close cooperation with infantry. Tigers were also used as a rear guard during German retreats, a role in which they were reported to be most successful. The British came to the conclusion that the use of this tank in an offensive role, even if supported by medium tanks, was discouraged.[289]

Overall, the Tiger did not make a very good impression on the British in North Africa, although there were some who saw its potential. R.A.C. Liaison Letter No.3 from the North African Forces issues a stern warning not to underestimate this new threat.

> "Owing to the fact that the Pzkw VI (Tiger) has on no occasion produced a decisive effect in any engagement, there is a danger that it may be belittled and written off as an unsuccessful freak vehicle unlikely to be met in large numbers.
>
> Any such attitude is to invite disaster.

---

[288] Canadian Military Headquarters, London (CMHQ), Files Block No. 55 - 5773, Image 1403

[289] Canadian Military Headquarters, London (CMHQ), Files Block No. 55 - 5773, Image 1403-1404

The PzKw VI has undoubtedly been used badly throughout the campaign, usually in small numbers and frequently with inadequate reconnaissance in front of it. In consequence it has fallen a victim to well sited defensive A.Tk guns trained to hold their fire until the tank was within close range.

It cannot be ignored that, while we have in the Sherman a tank that can compete on level or better with the PzKw III and IV of all types, in the PzKw VI the enemy has once again stolen the lead that he has held for nearly three years in gun power and in armor. There is every likelihood that PzKw VI will be met in increasing numbers in all future operations and prisoner reports indicate the production of an even heavier tank, PzKw VIII.

It has always been sufficiently realized[290] that in armored action quality is always as important and often more important than quantity.

There should therefore be no loss of time in producing a tank capable of competing at least on equal terms in armament and armor with, not only the best German tank now during the intervening time of production."[291]

---

[290] Despite commonly being associated with American spelling, "realized" is often found in British English as well.
[291] Army Ground Forces HQ Decimal Correspondence 470.8 - Tanks, Misc, *Excerpt, R.A.C. Liaison Letter No.3 from the North African Forces*

Study of Tiger #131

Tiger 131 was recovered on May 7th, 1943.[292] Inspection of the captured tank revealed a hull registration number of 250122 and turret registration number of 250639.[293] Information learned in this preliminary inspection of Tiger 131, analysis of another intact but not running Tiger, as well as study of Tiger wrecks in North Africa was compiled by Colonel W.M. Blagden, then the Deputy Director of Fighting Vehicles at the Ministry of Supply, into the *Special Report on German Pz.Kw.VI "Tiger"* dated June 5th, 1943. This report gave a fairly complete description of Germany's newest tank.

The tank was actually slightly larger than estimated: 20 feet 6 inches (6248 mm) long, 12 feet 3 inches (3734 mm) wide and 9 feet 5.5 inches (2883 mm) tall.[294] The hull of the Tiger was fully welded. This made the transmission impossible to access in any way short of removing the turret. There were no openings on the floor plate either.[295] While the hull had the same shape as seen on German tanks previously, the turret was different. The sides and rear of the turret were composed of one curved horseshoe-shaped plate. The opening in the horseshoe was covered with two narrow 100 mm thick frames, into which the gun was installed.[296]

Measurements of the track link widths were revised to 2 feet 5 inches (736 mm) for battle tracks and 1 foot 9 inches (533 mm) for transport tracks. There were 95 identical track links per track.[297] The report noted that there must have

---

[292] D. Oscroft, *The Myth of Tiger 131*, https://tankmuseum.org/article/the_myth_of_tiger_131, retrieved on November 6th, 2023

[293] Canadian Military Headquarters, London (CMHQ), Files Block No. 55 - 5773, Image 1391

[294] Canadian Military Headquarters, London (CMHQ), Files Block No. 55 - 5773, Image 1393

[295] Canadian Military Headquarters, London (CMHQ), Files Block No. 55 - 5775, Image 3632

[296] Canadian Military Headquarters, London (CMHQ), Files Block No. 55 - 5775, Image 3632

[297] Canadian Military Headquarters, London (CMHQ), Files Block No. 55 - 5773, Image 1392-1393

been some kind of defect in the track pin retaining rings, as a number of the rings were missing and their pins were floating freely.[298] The wheels of the tank were described as "Christie type" despite the torsion bar suspension. The wheels followed a complex interleaved system similar to what was used on German halftracks with 16 single bogie wheels and 4 double bogie wheels per side. To fit so many torsion bars in such a small space, the front bogie axles had to be tilted, with the right leaning backwards from the hull and the left leaning forwards. The front and rear wheels on each side were fitted with shock absorbers. There were no return rollers and the track returned along the top of the wheels.[299]

Maybach HL 210 TRM P45 engine used in the Tiger tank, Bovington Tank Museum. This was a powerful engine, but repeated failures during trials showed that it suffered from design defects. *(Peter Samsonov)*

---

[298] Canadian Military Headquarters, London (CMHQ), Files Block No. 55 - 5775, Image 3644

[299] Canadian Military Headquarters, London (CMHQ), Files Block No. 55 - 5773, Image 1397

The tank's engine was identified as a Maybach H.L.210 P.45 putting out 650 hp. The speedometer went up to 100 kph, although the top speed that could be achieved in trials on a road was 18 mph (29 kph).[300] An automatic fire extinguisher system was mounted in the engine compartment that could also be manually activated by the driver.[301] The engine was cooled by means of two radiators to its left and right. Air was pulled through each radiator by a pair of exhaust fans. The radiators were protected by louvers, but the report described the protection as incomplete, stating that it was likely that the radiators could be struck by shell splinters. However, this layout meant that burning fuel from Molotov cocktails or similar weapons entering the Tiger through the louvers would not make direct contact with the engine, limiting the damage it could cause. [302]

Tiger 131, Bovington Tank Museum. The mantlet of the Tiger tank was cast in a complex shape with thickened local sections, but the overall protection was unlikely to exceed the equivalent of 100 mm, same as the front of the hull. *(Peter Samsonov)*

---

[300] Canadian Military Headquarters, London (CMHQ), Files Block No. 55 - 5773, Image 1394
[301] Canadian Military Headquarters, London (CMHQ), Files Block No. 55 - 5773, Image 1397
[302] Canadian Military Headquarters, London (CMHQ), Files Block No. 55 - 5775, Image 3638

Armor thicknesses were the same as measured on wrecks previously, except the thickness of the gun mantlet was clarified. The mantlet plate was cast in one piece, generally 92 mm thick, but it was reinforced with a cylindrical mantlet behind it, bringing the total thickness around the gun sight to 150 mm and around the mounting of the main gun to 205 mm. However, the report notes that the effective strength of this kind of composite armor was unlikely to exceed a uniform plate 100 mm thick. No spaced armor or fittings for it were found, but track links were carried on the front to act as improvised armor as they were on other German tanks.[303]

The discussion of the tank's vulnerability did not stop at measuring the thickness of its armor. In part, the quality of the armor was brought up. While 100 mm thick front armor showed behavior similar to that of British I.T.80 plate, the 82 mm thick side armor both on the hull and the turret was of a much lower quality, with a strong tendency to crack and flake under fire. The quality of the cast gun mantlet was good. None were found that were penetrated or had cracked.[304] The report describes a number of penetration trials carried out against captured Tiger tanks. These trials will be covered in detail in a subsequent chapter.

As before, the report notes that there is no splash protection for the turret ring with the exception of meager coverage provided by raising the driver's visor. There was also no provision to prevent downwards ricochet from the gun mantlet into the relatively thin hull roof. Two cases were found where even a 75 mm shell penetrated by striking the bottom of the gun mantlet and deflecting downwards.[305]

---

[303] Canadian Military Headquarters, London (CMHQ), Files Block No. 55 - 5773, Image 1394
[304] Canadian Military Headquarters, London (CMHQ), Files Block No. 55 - 5775, Image 3633-3634
[305] Canadian Military Headquarters, London (CMHQ), Files Block No. 55 - 5775, Image 3633-3634

Tiger 131, Bovington Tank Museum. The location of the weld seam attaching the front of the hull to the side allows one to appreciate the thickness of the Tiger's armor. 100 mm of steel offered considerable protection and at the time of introduction far from every tank gun could penetrate this much armor. *(Peter Samsonov)*

Despite these weaknesses, there was no denying that this new tank was very well protected. Blagden proposed that a 17-pounder class gun was needed for effective AP attack. In the meantime, the tank could be stopped by destroying the wheels and tracks with HE fire from medium artillery[306] (4.5-5.5 inch guns and 6 inch howitzers[307]).

The tank followed typical practice already encountered on German medium tanks with carrying five crewmen: a driver and a radio operator/machine gunner in the hull and the commander, gunner, and loader in the turret. Since the 8.8 cm KwK 36 L/56 gun was a massive weapon and extended nearly the entire

---

[306] Canadian Military Headquarters, London (CMHQ), Files Block No. 55 - 5775, Image 3634

[307] N.F. Evans, *British Artillery in World War 2, Artillery Organisations*, https://nigelef.tripod.com/RAorg.htm, retrieved on January 11th, 2024

way to the rear of the turret ring, the commander couldn't sit behind the gun like on the Pz.Kpfw.III or Pz.Kpfw.IV. Instead, he was offset to the left, sitting behind the gunner. The commander's cupola was moved with him. Even though the commander and gunner occupied the larger of the two unequal halves created by the protruding gun, both positions were considered cramped.[308] The commander had three positions he could occupy. With the hatch opened up, he could sit on the upper seat for observation. With the hatch closed, he could either sit on the lower seat or stand on the turntable floor. All three positions were described as "cramped and uncomfortable".[309] The gunner had it even worse, as the leg shield cramped his position severely. The British considered his seat to be the most uncomfortable in the entire tank, although the position of the gun laying controls was good.[310]

Tiger 131, Bovington Tank Museum. The 8.8 cm KwK 36 was another key feature of the Tiger tank. The combination of thick armor and a long range gun made it a dangerous opponent. *(Peter Samsonov)*

The 8.8 cm KwK 36 gun installed in the tank was found to be similar to the Flak 36. The gun used in the tank was equipped with a double baffle muzzle brake and a semiautomatic vertical falling block breech. The gun was fired

---

[308] Canadian Military Headquarters, London (CMHQ), Files Block No. 55 - 5775, Image 3633
[309] Canadian Military Headquarters, London (CMHQ), Files Block No. 55 - 5773, Image 1707
[310] Canadian Military Headquarters, London (CMHQ), Files Block No. 55 - 5773, Image 1707

electrically with a button on the elevation handwheel. The coaxial MG-34 machine gun was fired with a foot pedal. Both were aimed using a T.Z.F.9b binocular sight. Few conclusions could be drawn about the properties of the sight since the lenses were missing.[311] The main gun could elevate to +15 degrees and depress to -9 degrees[312] (although the later report gives a depression of only -8 degrees)[313], however the clinometer carried in the tank was marked from +22.5 to -5.6 degrees. The MG-34 in the hull fired by the radio operator was aimed using the typical machine gun sight found in German tanks.[314] 92 rounds for the main gun were stowed in symmetrical compartments on each side of the tank: 32 rounds stowed on each side horizontally, 8 rounds stored on each side vertically, and 6 more rounds stowed under the fighting compartment floor horizontally on each side. The vertical compartment extended below the fighting compartment floor.[315]

The turret could be rotated manually by the gunner or by the commander. The gunner could also use the hydraulic powered traverse by means of a rocking plate operated with his feet. A lever could be used to set one of two speeds. The power traverse drew power from the driveshaft.[316] Even the powered traverse was considered to be rather slow. With the engine idling at 800 RPM, the powered traverse turned the turret at a speed of just 1.5 degrees per second in low gear and 3.5 degrees per second in high gear.[317] The massive gun was considerably out of balance, and even the system of levers with a compensating spring braced against the turret wall didn't prevent the gun from being difficult

---

[311] Canadian Military Headquarters, London (CMHQ), Files Block No. 55 - 5775, Image 3635
[312] Canadian Military Headquarters, London (CMHQ), Files Block No. 55 - 5773, Image 1395
[313] Canadian Military Headquarters, London (CMHQ), Files Block No. 55 - 5775, Image 3634
[314] Canadian Military Headquarters, London (CMHQ), Files Block No. 55 - 5773, Image 1395
[315] Canadian Military Headquarters, London (CMHQ), Files Block No. 55 - 5773, Image 1396
[316] Canadian Military Headquarters, London (CMHQ), Files Block No. 55 - 5773, Image 1395-1396
[317] Canadian Military Headquarters, London (CMHQ), Files Block No. 55 - 5775, Image 3646

to elevate but easy to depress.[318] Due to the size and weight of the gun and the turret, getting the gun on target was a slow process.[319]

The loader took the smaller right half of the turret, but he had it all to himself. Blagden notes that this extra space was very necessary due to the size of the ammunition. The loader needed all the space he could get to handle the 36.5 inch (93 cm) long rounds. His workspace was surrounded by ammunition bins, with another bin under his feet, accessible through a trapdoor when the turret was pointing directly forwards.[320] Getting the long and heavy rounds out of their bins in such a confined space was described as "very hard work".[321] For the loader's protection, the gun was equipped with an electric safety. Once the gun was loaded, the loader pushed a button, which enabled the firing circuit and lit up a lamp signaling to the gunner that the weapon was ready to fire. The same circuit prevented the gun from being fired if the gun was out of battery or if the recoil buffer was not filled with fluid.[322]

The Tiger tank was controlled by means of a handwheel and two skid brake levers. A fully regenerative steering system was used. Turning the tank with a handwheel was easy, but it took considerable strength to use the levers. The tank used a Maybach-Variorex pre-selector gearbox. Operation of the gearbox was quite complex, as despite there being 8 positions of the pre-selector, only four could be used depending on the gear range. A certain sequence of gears had to be followed when shifting, and it was not the same going up as going down. Failure to follow the sequence resulted in no change being made to the gear. Otherwise, the change came with "the delay and violent jerk that seems characteristic of this system". It was impossible to say more about the system

---

[318] Canadian Military Headquarters, London (CMHQ), Files Block No. 55 - 5775, Image 3635

[319] Canadian Military Headquarters, London (CMHQ), Files Block No. 55 - 5775, Image 3644

[320] Canadian Military Headquarters, London (CMHQ), Files Block No. 55 - 5775, Image 3633

[321] Canadian Military Headquarters, London (CMHQ), Files Block No. 55 - 5775, Image 3644

[322] Canadian Military Headquarters, London (CMHQ), Files Block No. 55 - 5775, Image 3633-3634

without disassembling it.³²³ The report notes that the complex steering system and large range of gears do a lot for the tank's mobility despite the poor power-to-weight ratio. No attempt was made to drive the tank off-road, so cross country performance was not evaluated. It was, however, noted that the tank's low clearance likely limits its mobility on uneven terrain, as several Tigers had been found that had bottomed out and thus could not be evacuated. The short contact length of the track with the ground that made the tank easier to steer was also expected to negatively impact stability and ground pressure. ³²⁴

One of the most interesting things noted about the Tiger tank was that it was sealed for underwater travel. All hatches had rubber seals and the turret ring was sealed with an inflatable rubber hose. The exhausts and air intakes of the engine compartment could also be sealed. The air intake seal was controlled with a switch labeled *"Wasserfahrt"* (water driving), leaving no doubt about the purpose of this feature. There was even a small bilge pump underneath the fighting compartment floor. During underwater travel, air would be taken in by a snorkel attached to the engine compartment and the crew would receive air through shutters in the bulkhead. No provision was found for supplying air directly into the crew compartment.³²⁵ In fact, air was only circulated through the tank by means of the engine exhaust, and if the engine were to stop while the tank was underwater the crew would suffocate.³²⁶ Blagden concludes that the presence of a deep wading system was a sign that the tank was developed for the invasion of Britain.³²⁷

The conclusion to Blagden's report describes the most important weaknesses of the Tiger's design. For all its armor and armament, it was much more

---

[323] Canadian Military Headquarters, London (CMHQ), Files Block No. 55 - 5775, Image 3641
[324] Canadian Military Headquarters, London (CMHQ), Files Block No. 55 - 5775, Image 3644
[325] Canadian Military Headquarters, London (CMHQ), Files Block No. 55 - 5773, Image 1398
[326] Canadian Military Headquarters, London (CMHQ), Files Block No. 55 - 5775, Image 3639
[327] Canadian Military Headquarters, London (CMHQ), Files Block No. 55 - 5775, Image 3644

complicated and expensive to produce than any of its predecessors and unlikely to be as common a threat as the lighter armed and armored German tanks.

> "The tank bristles with every sort of complication and one would think that it would be at least twice as difficult to produce as either of its predecessors. This may have a bearing on the numbers that are likely to be met with in the future and the degree of dilution by Mk. III's and IV's.
>
> It is extremely instructive to note the manner in which the Germans will face the problem of designing and producing a highly complicated mechanism in order to get functional perfection, rather than accept something less effective which the manufacturer would find easier or more desirable to produce. The relationship between state and industry in the Reich is evidently on a highly satisfactory footing."[328]

It is worth noting that the British analysis was entirely correct. The Tiger was tremendously expensive, even for its size and weight. Despite weighing just a third more than a Panther tank, the cost of a Tiger tank without armament was more than twice that of the Panther (250,800 vs 117,100 Reichsmarks respectively). While the cost of the chassis and turret were comparable (80,000 vs 76,000 Reichsmarks), 57% of the Tiger's final price paid for the assembly, compared to only 20-30% of the final cost of a Panther tank.[329]

---

[328] Canadian Military Headquarters, London (CMHQ), Files Block No. 55 - 5775, Image 3642

[329] J. Wehner, Waren deutsche Panzer zu teuer?, in: *Achtung Panzer? Zur Panzerwaffe der Wehrmacht*. Military History Group, 2022, p.49

Penetration Trials in North Africa

The Germans were not eager to abandon their newest, heaviest, and most expensive tank. For this reason, tanks that were abandoned were often located in quite precarious situations where recovery was just as difficult for the British as it was for the Germans. Nevertheless, the British had to make do. For this reason, the first penetration trials of a Tiger tank were carried out in quite confined conditions. The Tiger hull allocated for penetration trials was located in a minefield and could not be moved.[330] Traces of a small fire were discovered at the base of the tank, but it did not appear to have had any effect on the toughness of the armor.[331] A 100 yard (91 meter) long range was cleared by detonating some mines. Three vehicles were brought in to fire at the tank: a Sherman tank with a 75 mm M3 gun firing a APCBC M61 shell (striking velocity of 2020 f/s or 616 m/s at 100 yards), a Churchill III with a 57 mm 6-pdr Mk.III gun (already quite worn out with a striking velocity of 2220-2430 f/s or 677-741 m/s at 100 yards) firing AP shot with a low velocity charge, and a Churchill I or II tank with a 40 mm 2-pdr Mk.X gun (also worn out with a striking velocity of 2540-2640 f/s or 774-805 m/s at 100 yards) firing AP shot with a high velocity charge. Trials were conducted on May 19th, 1943.[332]

---

[330] Canadian Military Headquarters, London (CMHQ), Files Block No. 55 - 5775, Image 3648
[331] Canadian Military Headquarters, London (CMHQ), Files Block No. 55 - 5775, Image 3649
[332] Canadian Military Headquarters, London (CMHQ), Files Block No. 55 - 5775, Image 3648

Medium Tank M4 or Sherman I in British nomenclature, Overloon War Museum. Its 75 mm gun performed splendidly against the latest German tanks at El Alamein, but was only useful against the Tiger at short range from the side. *(Peter Samsonov)*

The Sherman was the first to fire. The 62 mm thick lower side armor was penetrated at an angle of 30 degrees from normal. A flake dislodged from the back of the armor. Against the upper 82 mm thick side, a hit at 30 degrees only produced a scoop with a slight bulge on the rear side. Several more shots established that the critical angle of penetration at 100 yards was 17.5 degrees. Penetrations resulted in irregular jagged holes. The round that penetrated at an angle of 16.5 degrees dislodged quite a large flake, 11x6" (279x152 mm).[333]

The Churchill III with a 6-pounder gun was next. The shot shattered when impacting at an angle from 30 degrees all the way down to 5 degrees. It was impossible to hit the plate at a smaller angle due to the fact that the Tiger under

---

[333] Canadian Military Headquarters, London (CMHQ), Files Block No. 55 - 5775, Image 3648

trial was tilted.³³⁴ This was unexpected, as other Tigers with holes from 6-pounder guns have previously been found.³³⁵ The results were discarded owing to the worn out gun and low quality of the particular batch of ammunition.³³⁶

Churchill III tank, Canadian War Museum. The 57 mm 6-pounder gun on this tank performed poorly in this trial, although the effect was blamed on the worn barrel and low quality of the particular batch of ammunition used. *(Peter Samsonov)*

The Churchill with a 2-pounder gun went last. Firing at 5 degrees or as close to normal as possible, the 40 mm shot penetrated three bogey wheels but failed

---

³³⁴ Canadian Military Headquarters, London (CMHQ), Files Block No. 55 - 5775, Image 3649
³³⁵ Canadian Military Headquarters, London (CMHQ), Files Block No. 55 - 5775, Image 3633
³³⁶ Canadian Military Headquarters, London (CMHQ), Files Block No. 55 - 5775, Image 3634

to penetrate the main armor. A second shot hit clear of any wheels and lodged in the plate, displacing a flake from the back.[337]

Churchill II tank with a 40 mm 2-pounder gun, Bovington Tank Museum. The 2-pounder could only damage a Tiger if it hit the side armor clear of the road wheels. (Peter Samsonov)

The British concluded that some surface hardening must have been performed on account of the shatter of 6-pdr AP shot as it was unlikely to shatter against homogeneous plate at this velocity and angle of impact. The jagged holes produced by 75 mm shells confirmed this theory. Barring the flaking, the resistance to penetration of the plates under test was higher than that of British I.T.80D plate.[338]

---

[337] Canadian Military Headquarters, London (CMHQ), Files Block No. 55 - 5775, Image 3649
[338] Canadian Military Headquarters, London (CMHQ), Files Block No. 55 - 5775, Image 3649

More thorough trials were carried out against a different tank near Bon Ficha, Tunisia, from July 30th to August 3rd, 1943. A 75 mm M3 gun in a Sherman tank and a 6-pounder were used once again (this time a towed Mk.II). Instead of a 2-pounder, a 17-pounder was used. Unlike in the previous trials, the guns were almost new. A larger variety of ranges was simulated by adjusting the amount of propellant. The target chosen was a Tiger tank hull recovered from a workshop. The turret and all internal fittings were removed. There was no sign of fire damage and all battle damage was limited to the port side, making it a prime target for testing.[339]

Ordnance QF 6-pounder gun Mk.II, Musée des Blindés, Saumur. This 57 mm anti-tank gun could even penetrate the front armor of the Tiger tank. *(Peter Samsonov)*

The 6-pounder fired first. The new 6-pounder performed much better than the worn one used in previous trials. 57 mm AP and APC shot remained whole even if they failed to penetrate the armor. The German plate, on the other hand, performed poorly, giving large flakes when penetrated.[340] At normal, the

---

[339] WO 194/744, *Firing trial in Tunisia against the hull of German Pz Kw VI Tiger tank*, p.2
[340] WO 194/744, *Firing trial in Tunisia against the hull of German Pz Kw VI Tiger tank*, p.3

vulnerable range of the 82 mm thick starboard side armor was found to be 1300 yards (1189 m) when using a high velocity 6-pounder and 975 yards when using a lower velocity variant of the gun. This was equivalent to 80-86 mm of British armor.[341] At an angle of 30 degrees from normal, both AP and APC shot shattered without penetration.[342]

The port side held up much worse. It flaked very badly when hit with AP shot, dislodging flakes up to 10 inches (254 mm) in diameter.[343] The ballistic limit was not established, but the W/R limit[344] suggested that the tank would have been vulnerable to the longer 6-pounder from over 1650 yards (1509 m) and the shorter gun from over 1300 yards (1189 m). This was equivalent to just 65 mm of British armor, despite the German plate being 82 mm thick. The British shot still shattered when impacting at 30 degrees even against this low quality armor.[345]

The rear plate, also 82 mm thick, could only be shot from an angle of 20 degrees. This plate performed better than the sides, only giving one flake 4 inches (102 mm) in diameter.[346] The ballistic limit was established as equivalent to 1050 yards (960 m) for the longer 6-pounder and 750 yards (686 m) for the shorter weapon.[347]

---

[341] WO 194/744, *Firing trial in Tunisia against the hull of German Pz Kw VI Tiger tank*, p.5
[342] WO 194/744, *Firing trial in Tunisia against the hull of German Pz Kw VI Tiger tank*, p.3
[343] WO 194/744, *Firing trial in Tunisia against the hull of German Pz Kw VI Tiger tank*, p.4
[344] Limit between a velocity sufficient to put the shell or shot clean through the armor (W) and sufficient to penetrate the armor and lodge the shell in it (R).
[345] WO 194/744, *Firing trial in Tunisia against the hull of German Pz Kw VI Tiger tank*, p.5
[346] WO 194/744, *Firing trial in Tunisia against the hull of German Pz Kw VI Tiger tank*, p.4
[347] WO 194/744, *Firing trial in Tunisia against the hull of German Pz Kw VI Tiger tank*, p.5

A privately owned 6-pounder Mk.IV anti-tank gun displayed during Aquino Tank Weekend at the Ontario Regiment Museum. This variant had a longer barrel than the Mk.II, resulting in higher muzzle velocity and superior penetration. *(Peter Samsonov)*

The 6-pounder was also used against the front of the Tiger. The driver's visor plate (102 mm tilted at 10 degrees) did not show any flaking or cracking under fire, but it could still be penetrated. Only two shots were fired at the lower front armor (102 mm at 25 degrees), one of which ricocheted and one of which shattered on impact.[348] The ballistic limit against the driver's visor armor was established to be 800 yards (732 m) for the high velocity 6-pounder and 500 yards (457 m) for the low velocity gun.[349]

The Sherman's 75 mm gun was used second, although not as extensively as the 6-pounder. M61 APCBC shells were fired at the stronger starboard side. As with the 6-pounder, large flakes were dislodged on impact up to 4.5" (114 mm) in diameter. The seventh shot knocked out a piece of plate 2 feet by 1 foot (710

---

[348] WO 194/744, *Firing trial in Tunisia against the hull of German Pz Kw VI Tiger tank*, p.4
[349] WO 194/744, *Firing trial in Tunisia against the hull of German Pz Kw VI Tiger tank*, p.5

by 305 mm).³⁵⁰ The W/R limit of 1706 f/s (520 m/s) meant that the plate was vulnerable at a range of up to 900 yards (823 m).³⁵¹

Since the side armor did not present a considerable challenge for the 76 mm 17-pounder, it was only fired at the strongest part of the tank: the sloped lower front armor. The plate plugged badly under attack by 17-pounder AP shot. The projectiles also performed badly, shattering into large pieces on impact. Ironically, this increased the damage that would have been done to the insides of the tank, as in some cases even if the base of the shot lodged in the armor, the noses broke off and flew into the tank.³⁵² However, the armor was still defeated at velocities equivalent to ranges of up to 2050 yards (1875 m), which was equal to about 103 mm of British armor.³⁵³

A privately owned early 17-pounder gun on a 25-pounder carriage displayed during Tankfest at the Bovington Tank Museum. The 17-pounder could defeat the Tiger's armor at a long range, even if the quality of the AP shot left something to be desired. (Peter Samsonov)

---

[350] WO 194/744, *Firing trial in Tunisia against the hull of German Pz Kw VI Tiger tank*, p.4
[351] WO 194/744, *Firing trial in Tunisia against the hull of German Pz Kw VI Tiger tank*, p.5
[352] WO 194/744, *Firing trial in Tunisia against the hull of German Pz Kw VI Tiger tank*, p.8
[353] WO 194/744, *Firing trial in Tunisia against the hull of German Pz Kw VI Tiger tank*, p.5

Aside from the one plate that showed considerably poorer ballistic resistance than British plate, German armor resisted attack more or less as well as British I.T.80D plate. However, when it failed, "the mode of failure was both more sudden and more disastrous" than with British armor. All plates plugged badly under fire. And even the two plates that were closer in quality to British standards cracked and flaked when hit. 102 mm thick front armor was less likely to flake, but plugged just as badly as the sides. However, penetrations on Tiger hulls inspected on the battlefield suggested that the front of the tank was just as variable in quality as the sides turned out to be.[354]

The report on penetration trials ended on a high note.

> "If the armor tested so far is typical of recent German production, the outlook is distinctly encouraging. There is nothing like the same consistently high quality that was found in specimens of the thinner German machineable quality armor taken from the Pz.Kw.III and Pz.Kw.IV. The hardness of the thicker plates does not materially increase their ballistic resistance above that of softer British armor, hence there is no compensation for the worse behaviour of the German plates when overmatched."[355]

At the same time, it was noted that the quality and performance of 6-pounder and 17-pounder AP shot left much to be desired. Large scale trials of AP, APC, and APCBC shot against either German armor or British armor treated to a comparable hardness were recommended.[356]

---

[354] WO 194/744, *Firing trial in Tunisia against the hull of German Pz Kw VI Tiger tank*, p.7
[355] WO 194/744, *Firing trial in Tunisia against the hull of German Pz Kw VI Tiger tank*, p.7
[356] WO 194/744, *Firing trial in Tunisia against the hull of German Pz Kw VI Tiger tank*, pp.8-9

Observation from the Tiger

In the search for weaknesses of the Tiger tank, a separate study was made of its vision devices.

The commander of the Tiger tank was equipped with a cupola. The cupola had five slits covered by triplex blocks. Unlike in earlier German tanks, there were no armored shields that could be lowered to protect the slits when not in use. The report theorized that this was done because the shields easily became jammed in the African sand. The front vision block had a sighting vane to show where the turret was pointing.[357] A pistol port was also available behind the commander at the 8 o'clock position.[358]

Tiger 131, Bovington Tank Museum. The commander's cupola of the Tiger tank proved unsatisfactory due to its poor placement, vision slits that required a great deal of head movement to use, and a cramped commander's workspace that made turning around to look backwards difficult. *(Peter Samsonov)*

The position of the commander to the left of the center of the tank severely compromised his vision to the point where the report author concluded that designers of the Tiger "did not consider near vision to be so important". While Pz.Kpfw.III and Pz.Kpfw.IV tanks were considered to have good vision due to the central position of their cupolas and sloping of the roof that minimized blind

---

[357] Canadian Military Headquarters, London (CMHQ), Files Block No. 55 - 5775, Image 3635-3636
[358] Canadian Military Headquarters, London (CMHQ), Files Block No. 55 - 5773, Image 1707

spots, the fact that the Tiger's cupola was shifted to the left meant that a large blind spot to the right and right rear was introduced. Additionally, the lack of shutters meant that the slit for the vision blocks had to be as narrow as possible. This meant that the commander could not see the full field of view of any given slit without moving his head around. Without head movement, there was a 15-20 degree blind spot between each vision block. Movement was also made difficult by the commander's cramped position which made turning to look to the rear difficult. The large stowage bin behind the turret also created a large blind spot in that direction.[359]

Tiger 131, Bovington Tank Museum. Openings for the gunner's gun sight and the vision slit pointing left. The British considered that more vision devices pointing forward would be more useful for the gunner. *(Peter Samsonov)*

The gunner's primary means of observation was through a T.Z.F.9b binocular telescope with a 23 degree field of view.[360] The gunner and loader had two identical lookouts at 10 and 2 o'clock. The loader had the same pistol port as the commander at 4 o'clock.[361] The loader's vision block covered a portion of the

---

[359] Canadian Military Headquarters, London (CMHQ), Files Block No. 55 - 5773, Image 1708
[360] Canadian Military Headquarters, London (CMHQ), Files Block No. 55 - 5773, Image 1710
[361] Canadian Military Headquarters, London (CMHQ), Files Block No. 55 - 5775, Image 3636

commander's blind spot.[362] Unfortunately, considerable head movement was also required to obtain a full range of view from this device, and the loader was limited in how much he could see by the location of his kit bin. The loader's position was described as "uncomfortably blind" in the report. The report notes that newer models of the Tiger had an escape hatch instead of the rear pistol port and also added a fixed periscope for the loader to look through.[363]

Tiger 131, Bovington Tank Museum. The loader's vision slit on the opposite side of the turret. It somewhat made up for one of the blind spots of the commander's cupola, but the placement of nearby stowage made it impossible for the loader to make full use of its range of vision. *(Peter Samsonov)*

---

[362] Canadian Military Headquarters, London (CMHQ), Files Block No. 55 - 5773, Image 1708
[363] Canadian Military Headquarters, London (CMHQ), Files Block No. 55 - 5773, Image 1710

The hull gunner had a K.Z.F.2 optical sight on the machine gun ball mount giving a field of view of 18 degrees.[364] A fixed periscope was installed in his hatch, pointing about 30 degrees to the right.[365]

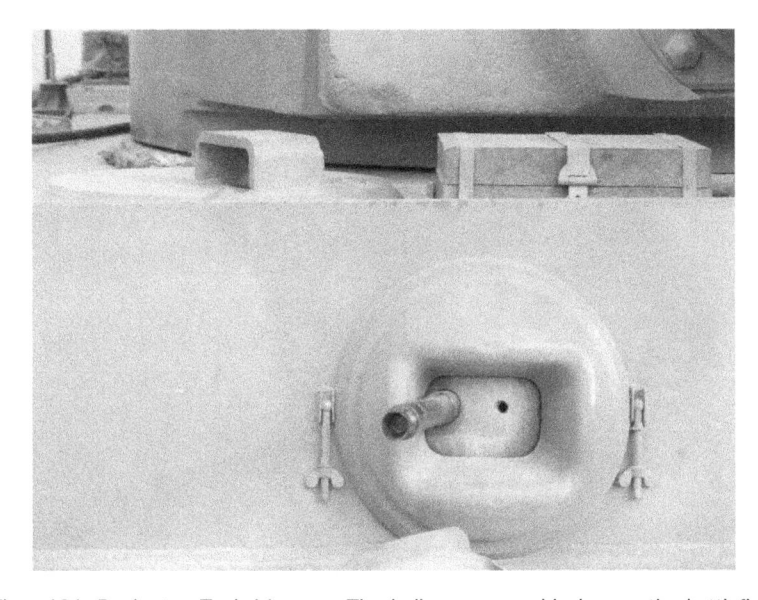

Tiger 131, Bovington Tank Museum. The hull gunner could observe the battlefield through his machine gun sight and the fixed periscope in his hatch. *(Peter Samsonov)*

The driver had a triplex visor block to look through. Unlike the blocks in the commander's cupola, this one could be covered by a shutter. There was also a K.F.F.2 periscopic device for driving with the shutter closed, but some tanks had this equipment removed and the holes for it welded up. In addition, the driver had a fixed periscope in his hatch pointing about 30 degrees to the left.[366] The

---

[364] Canadian Military Headquarters, London (CMHQ), Files Block No. 55 - 5773, Image 1710

[365] Canadian Military Headquarters, London (CMHQ), Files Block No. 55 - 5775, Image 3636

[366] Canadian Military Headquarters, London (CMHQ), Files Block No. 55 - 5775, Image 3636

driver's position is the only one described as having "good and adequate vision".³⁶⁷

Tiger 131, Bovington Tank Museum. In addition to his main vision block, the driver had a fixed periscope in his hatch like the hull gunner. There was also a secondary vision device that allowed some forward vision with the shutter closed, but on Tiger 131 it was removed and its openings welded shut. *(Peter Samsonov)*

The report suggested that tank hunters approaching the Tiger from the right or right rear would become invisible to the crew at a range of 100-120 feet (30.5-36.6 meters). This was largely due to the sizable blind spot created by the location and layout of the commander's station. Even though the loader's vision block partially covered this blind spot, the position of other equipment in the tank limited his use of it.³⁶⁸

---

³⁶⁷ Canadian Military Headquarters, London (CMHQ), Files Block No. 55 - 5773, Image 1710
³⁶⁸ Canadian Military Headquarters, London (CMHQ), Files Block No. 55 - 5773, Image 1708

Testing the Gun

The British also tested the gun of their captured Tiger. The volume of the trials was limited by a fracture of the front right suspension arm, meaning that the tank was stuck at the range and could not move towards or away from its targets.[369] Interestingly enough, the engine had also failed during gunnery trials. Inspection showed that failure of end bearings caused considerable damage to crank pins. The same failure was found on two other Tiger engines, suggesting that this was a weakness of the design.[370]

It was noted that the Germans used a flashless propellant that indeed produced no flash while firing in daylight, but produced a lot of smoke.[371] The smoke was dispersed to the sides by the muzzle brake to some extent, but even though a wind helped clear the smoke during the trials the gunner could not observe his shots landing at a range of under 1600 yards (1463 m). The commander could see over the smoke cloud in most cases.[372] Due to a shortage of Tiger ammunition, Flak ammunition equipped with electric primers was also used in the trials. This worked, but the Flak rounds gave a large muzzle flash and also a large backflash in 3 out of 4 cases even in conditions that were not conducive to backflash. This confirmed the British theory that the large shield next to the commander was there to protect him from backflash and that backflash was likely the cause of the Germans adopting flashless ammunition for the Tiger.[373]

Tracking trials were next. While British tanks of the time had either an electric motor or an electrically powered hydraulic pump driving the powered traverse,

---

[369] Canadian Military Headquarters, London (CMHQ), Files Block No. 55 - 5773, Image 1713
[370] Canadian Military Headquarters, London (CMHQ), Files Block No. 55 - 5773, Image 1762
[371] Canadian Military Headquarters, London (CMHQ), Files Block No. 55 - 5773, Image 1711
[372] Canadian Military Headquarters, London (CMHQ), Files Block No. 55 - 5773, Image 1712
[373] Canadian Military Headquarters, London (CMHQ), Files Block No. 55 - 5773, Image 1711-1712

the Tiger's hydraulic pump was powered from the engine driveshaft. This unusual system was tested thoroughly.

A target moving at 15 mph (24 kph) at 1000 yards (914 m) was tracked by the Tiger. It was easy to track in low gear, but the dead zone of the powered traverse controls was very large.[374] There was also no definite neutral position for the rocking plate controlling the turret traverse; it was hard to tell when the plate returned to the center when the gunner wished to stop turning the turret.[375] It was harder to track in high gear since the traverse speed was irregular. This mode was unsuitable for targets at a range of 1000 yards (914 m) moving at a speed of 5 mph (8 kph) and required correction by hand for tracking targets moving at 10 mph (16 kph). It was easy to traverse the turret by hand.

The trial did not just involve tracking, but also firing. Five rounds were fired at a target moving at 15 mph (24 kph) at a range of 1500 yards (1372 m). The gunner aimed with a combination of low speed power traverse and hand traverse. Smoke from the gun obscured the target from the gunner, but with the commander's aid 3 out of 5 shots hit their target.[376]

The Tiger showed itself to be a stable firing platform. The gun rose for the first two or three rounds after stopping as the suspension settled. After the gunner was guided onto a target at 1100 yards (1006 m) he could fire five shots and hit without the need to adjust his aim. At a range of 1200 yards (1097 m) all shots in a group of five landed in an area 16x18 inches (406x457 mm). A target was

---

[374] Canadian Military Headquarters, London (CMHQ), Files Block No. 55 - 5773, Image 1713
[375] Canadian Military Headquarters, London (CMHQ), Files Block No. 55 - 5773, Image 1714
[376] Canadian Military Headquarters, London (CMHQ), Files Block No. 55 - 5773, Image 1713

also engaged at a range of 1800 yards (1646 m) with the aid of a clinometer.[377] Using normal bracketing methods[378], a hit was scored on the 4th shot.[379]

The peak rate of fire (with the first round already loaded) was 4 rounds over the course of 39 seconds. It was estimated that the normal rate of fire was 5-8 RPM. The testers appreciated that the Tiger retained a high rate of fire over time as more rounds were readily accessible from the loader's station than in their own heavy tanks.[380] However, the rate of fire was reduced due to the fact that the rounds were front-heavy and stored in a way that this imbalance made them difficult to pick up.[381]

Without the ability to run the engine, the quality of air had to be analyzed with just the ventilation fan running. The concentration of ammonia (NH_3) in the tank reached 150 ppm after two shots and 191 at the end of a 5 round burst. The fumes were found to exit the fighting compartment slowly, the concentration of carbon monoxide (CO) was dangerously high, and the amount of ammonia in the air was irritating.[382]

---

[377] A clinometer is a device showing the elevation of the gun, allowing a tank to engage a target using artillery tables rather than the gun sight.

[378] Bracketing is an artillery technique where range to a target can be estimated by overshooting one round, undershooting a second round, and observing the target's relative location between the two points of impact.

[379] Canadian Military Headquarters, London (CMHQ), Files Block No. 55 - 5773, Image 1713

[380] Canadian Military Headquarters, London (CMHQ), Files Block No. 55 - 5773, Image 1713
This most likely refers to the Churchill tank, but the exact model of British heavy tank the report author had in mind is not specified in the text.

[381] Canadian Military Headquarters, London (CMHQ), Files Block No. 55 - 5773, Image 1711

[382] Canadian Military Headquarters, London (CMHQ), Files Block No. 55 - 5773, Image 1711

Rematch in Italy

The encounter with Tiger tanks in North Africa was far from the last for British and American forces. After the Afrika Korps surrendered and the Allies gained control of the Mediterranean, the time came to move the fighting further north, to Sicily. Here, the Allies would face off against the 2nd company of the *schwere Panzer Abteilung* 504, originally meant to be sent to North Africa. 17 Tiger tanks were still in Sicily by July 1943, 15 of which were ready for service on the day of the Allied invasion on July 10th. These Tigers did not last long.[383] The company was down to twelve Tigers by the end of day on July 12th, six by the end of July 13th, and just four Tigers by the end of July 14th. The remaining Tigers retreated west towards Etna, where three out of the four had to be demolished. The last Tiger (turret number 222) was transported to mainland Italy, but broke down and also had to be demolished.[384] All Tiger tanks in Sicily were encountered by American forces. The Americans took many photographs of the wrecks and recovered two Tiger tanks, one with turret number 211 and one without a turret number. Both were shipped to New York. However, it seemed that there was no rush to study the tank. The first photograph taken in Sicily was only published in an American intelligence bulletin in January 1945 and then in the *Handbook on German Military Forces* in March of 1945.[385] The author is not aware of any detailed studies conducted with these tanks.

After the sole Tiger from *schwere Panzer-Abteilung* 504, *schwere Panzer-Abteilung* 508 was next to arrive in mainland Italy.[386] The battalion received its Tigers by the end of January 1944[387] and made it to the beachheads at Anzio by February 16th.[388] This was not an easy journey for the Tigers. The steep slopes and sharp turns of the mountain roads were a challenge for both the drivers and their equipment. One Tiger tank even caught fire and exploded en route to the front lines. About 60% of the Tigers broke down during the 200 km

---

[383] B.O. Newsome, *The Tiger Tank and Allied Intelligence Volume III, Tiger 131: From Africa to Europe*, Tank Archives Press, Coronado, 2020, pp.97-98

[384] W. Schneider, *Tigers in Combat I*, Stackpole Books, Mechanicsburg, 2004, p.196

[385] B.O. Newsome, *The Tiger Tank and Allied Intelligence Volume III, Tiger 131: From Africa to Europe*, Tank Archives Press, Coronado, 2020, pp.98-101

[386] C.W. Wilbeck, Sledgehammers Strengths and Flaws of Tiger Tank Battalions in World War II, The Aberjona Press, Bedford, 2004, p.86

[387] W. Schneider, *Tigers in Combat I*, Stackpole Books, Mechanicsburg, 2004, p.321

[388] W. Schneider, *Tigers in Combat I*, Stackpole Books, Mechanicsburg, 2004, p.322

march and the battalion arrived at Anzio piecemeal instead of as one decisive force. Once on location, the Tigers were constrained by the swampy terrain and forced to operate on roads. This constraint proved fatal to the Tigers, as they could not maneuver around mines or avoid artillery that had dialed in on their position.[389] To make matters worse, German recovery vehicles were unarmored, making recovery of even lightly damaged Tiger tanks difficult and dangerous. As a result, the attempt to use Tiger tanks to crush the Anzio beachhead on February 29th failed.[390] Only four Tigers were written off as total losses, but *schwere Panzer-Abteilung* 508's fighting strength was severely sapped. 32 tanks were reported operational on February 29th, 1944, and only 12 on March 1st. The remaining Tigers returned to Rome.[391]

The *schwere Panzer-Abteilung* 508 took part in some smaller scale operations. Several tanks were employed in an indirect fire role in mid-April.[392] Tigers continued to give mechanical trouble and vehicles had to be abandoned as the Germans were forced to retreat.[393] The last large action in which the *schwere Panzer-Abteilung* 508 was involved took place in the vicinity of Cisterna on May 23rd-24th.

This attack could be considered a success, but the success was small and limited. The Americans were driven back by 3 kilometers in one sector[394] and the Germans claimed the destruction of 15 American tanks, but the cost was very high. One Tiger was lost to enemy artillery fire, one to transmission trouble, and two more to running gear issues. Another tank was lost when 3rd company of *schwere Panzer-Abteilung* 508 crossed a steep embankment where the Tigers' long barrels scraped the ground and thus had to be cleaned immediately. While stationary, the tanks came under artillery fire and the radiator of one Tiger was

---

[389] C.W. Wilbeck, *Sledgehammers Strengths and Flaws of Tiger Tank Battalions in World War II*, The Aberjona Press, Bedford, 2004, p.87

[390] C.W. Wilbeck, *Sledgehammers Strengths and Flaws of Tiger Tank Battalions in World War II*, The Aberjona Press, Bedford, 2004, p.91

[391] W. Schneider, *Tigers in Combat I*, Stackpole Books, Mechanicsburg, 2004, p.322

[392] C.W. Wilbeck, *Sledgehammers Strengths and Flaws of Tiger Tank Battalions in World War II*, The Aberjona Press, Bedford, 2004, p.92

[393] W. Schneider, *Tigers in Combat I*, Stackpole Books, Mechanicsburg, 2004, pp.322-323

[394] C.W. Wilbeck, *Sledgehammers Strengths and Flaws of Tiger Tank Battalions in World War II*, The Aberjona Press, Bedford, 2004, p.92

destroyed, forcing the crew to retreat to Cori in short stages as their tank's engine overheated. This was not the end of the Tigers' troubles. When trying to evacuate the three Tigers that broke down, four out of the six tanks allocated for this mission experienced transmission trouble themselves. The three Tigers that were being towed had to be demolished and more Tigers allocated to tow the freshly broken ones. Only eight Tigers returned to Cori in addition to the one with a perforated radiator, four of which were in fighting order. Of those four, two promptly went out of action due to transmission trouble and one was damaged by artillery. By the night of May 24-25th the sole remaining Tiger had also broken down and had to be towed away by two captured Sherman tanks. As it was impossible to get engineering halftracks through to evacuate the Tigers, all nine tanks that reached the assembly point at Cori were demolished.[395] The *schwere Panzer-Abteilung* 508 was recalled to Rome and the battalion commander was relieved of duty.[396]

After its destruction in North Africa, *schwere Panzer-Abteilung* 504 was reconstituted by the end of 1943. The newly formed battalion received its Tiger tanks by April 21st, 1944.[397] It was deployed in Italy on June 20th, 1944, just in time to take part in a withdrawal to Rome. As the *schwere Panzer-Abteilung* 508, it managed to fight an effective delaying action against the American 1st Armored Division, resulting in the abandonment of 12 Sherman tanks and destruction of 11 on June 22nd. However, the Americans were able to outmaneuver the sluggish German tanks in the difficult terrain and continue their advance. Forced to retreat, the *schwere Panzer-Abteilung* 504 abandoned 28 of its 45 Tiger tanks between June 22nd and July 1st, 1944. Even relatively minor battle damage or breakdown turned into a total loss, as the Germans did not have the ability to evacuate their Tigers fast enough. Their opponents, however, had two full engineering companies that could not only evacuate damaged tanks, but also build bridges, improve fords, and clear rubble in order to keep up the pace of the American advance. Only 27 Tiger tanks made it to Cecina, 10 from *schwere Panzer-Abteilung* 508 and 17 from *schwere Panzer-Abteilung* 504.[398]

---

[395] C.W. Wilbeck, *Sledgehammers Strengths and Flaws of Tiger Tank Battalions in World War II*, The Aberjona Press, Bedford, 2004, pp.93-94
[396] W. Schneider, *Tigers in Combat I*, Stackpole Books, Mechanicsburg, 2004, p.323
[397] W. Schneider, *Tigers in Combat I*, Stackpole Books, Mechanicsburg, 2004, p.159
[398] C.W. Wilbeck, *Sledgehammers Strengths and Flaws of Tiger Tank Battalions in World War II*, The Aberjona Press, Bedford, 2004, pp.95-97

Both sides took note of these dramatic losses. Captured German documents contained a call to preserve Tiger tanks. Commanders were encouraged to consider whether or not the same mission could be done just as well with other weapons and reminded that every Tiger tank costs the German people 300,000 work hours.[399] It is worth noting that this value was likely inflated and the Tiger never took more than 180,000 work hours to manufacture.[400] Another memo reminded commanders that even a Tiger tank cannot "prance around oblivious of the laws of tank tactics", urging commanders to not demand the impossible of Tiger tanks.[401]

The British made their own assessment on the deployment of Tiger tanks. Since this was the first time Tigers were seen operating in large numbers, the battles in Italy were analyzed closely. The British noted that, for the most part, Tigers fought from ambushes. Both the approach to the ambush position and the position itself were covered with foliage. The Tigers would fire a few rounds from the ambush and move to another position. Tigers rarely fought alone. There were almost always other tanks and SPGs and sometimes infantry protecting their flanks. Very careful reconnaissance was required when one was deploying towed anti-tank guns or tank destroyers against a Tiger, as the vehicles or infantry protecting the Tiger remained concealed until they were needed. The British recommended allowing as much time as possible for reconnaissance when engaging Tigers.

Despite German memos urging caution, Tiger commanders were overconfident in their vehicles and attacked "almost recklessly", often breaking away from their supporting elements. At the same time, Tigers were very sensitive to artillery. The start of a barrage would invariably cause a Tiger to withdraw, as its commander was no doubt aware of how difficult it would be to evacuate and repair the tank. In one instance, two 75 mm smoke shells followed by AP fired by Sherman tanks was enough to force a Tiger to withdraw. Even if a gun that could penetrate the Tiger's armor was not available, this was still

---

[399] Canadian Military Headquarters, London (CMHQ), Files Block No. 55 - 5776, Image 19

[400] J. Wehner, Waren deutsche Panzer zu teuer?, in: *Achtung Panzer? Zur Panzerwaffe der Wehrmacht*. Military History Group, 2022, p.48

[401] Canadian Military Headquarters, London (CMHQ), Files Block No. 55 - 5777, Image 2198

recommended as a method for scaring off Tigers. The British also noted that the Tiger was slow to bring its gun on target, so simultaneous frontal and flank attack was recommended.[402]

Several examples of engagements with Tiger tanks were also provided. In one case, a Tiger tank was spotted at a range of 3000 yards (2743 m) engaging three Sherman tanks. A 17-pounder anti tank gun was brought up to fire at the tank's side from a range of 2400 yards (2195 m). No penetrating hits were scored from this range, but when the Tiger swung its turret around to fire at the 17-pounder, it exposed the thinner turret side to the Shermans, who were just 500 yards (457 m) away. After taking fire from the Shermans, the Tiger withdrew.[403]

In another engagement, a Tiger tank under artillery fire was abandoned by its crew for an unknown reason. The tank could not be examined, as shortly after one of the crewmen returned despite the ongoing shelling and drove away in his tank. There were other cases where Tigers under fire left seemingly good positions and withdrew even when there was no observed indication that they had taken any serious damage.[404] Upon taking fire from a 25-pounder artillery gun, one Tiger tank reversed and lodged itself in a house, after which it was abandoned.[405]

A study titled "Who Killed Tiger?" was attached to the Mediterranean Area AFV Technical Report No.23 for October 1944. The fact that a large number of Tiger tanks were abandoned between Anzio and Rome did not go unnoticed, and a detailed study of 12 wrecks was conducted. For the most part, the tanks did not show battle damage, and those with penetrations of their hull were likely to have sustained that damage after they were abandoned. Most tanks had damaged suspensions and running gear. A number either had no obvious cause

---

[402] Canadian Military Headquarters, London (CMHQ), Files Block No. 55 - 5777, Image 2116
[403] Canadian Military Headquarters, London (CMHQ), Files Block No. 55 - 5777, Image 2117
[404] Canadian Military Headquarters, London (CMHQ), Files Block No. 55 - 5777, Image 2117
[405] Canadian Military Headquarters, London (CMHQ), Files Block No. 55 - 5776, Image 567

for abandonment or were damaged to such a degree by a demolition charge that no cause could be determined. Broken tow ropes suggested that attempts to tow broken and bogged down tanks were not uncommon. Interrogation of a POW confirmed that these were the aforementioned tanks from 3rd company of the *schwere Panzer-Abteilung* 508 tasked with stopping the Allied breakthrough at Anzio, broken down and abandoned during the retreat to Cori.[406]

A late production Tiger tank, Musée des Blindés, Saumur. A number of improvements were made to the Tiger's design throughout its service life, but fundamental issues with reliability were never resolved. *(Peter Samsonov)*

---

[406] Canadian Military Headquarters, London (CMHQ), Files Block No. 55 - 5776, Image 630

Tiger 131, Bovington Tank Museum. Tropical air filters were installed on Tiger tanks for additional filtration of dust from air entering the engine. Even this setup was considered unsatisfactory by British standards. *(Peter Samsonov)*

The report concluded that the greatest danger to the Tiger tank in Italy was the Tiger itself.

> "Tiger is not yet sufficiently developed to be considered a reliable vehicle for long marches.
>
> He suffers from frequent suspension defects and probably, also gearbox trouble.
>
> When pushed, as in a retreat, these troubles are too frequent and serious for the German maintenance and recovery organization to deal with.
>
> Tiger killed himself."[407]

---

[407] Canadian Military Headquarters, London (CMHQ), Files Block No. 55 - 5776, Image 631

Subsequent reports noted that the retreat from Anzio to Cori was not an outlier. Tigers abandoned due to mechanical damage were a recurring sight.[408] In part, this could be due to the heat and dust that characterized the Italian theater of war. An examination of the two-stage "tropical" air filters taken from Tiger 131 by the Department of Tank Design came to the conclusion that the cleaners became obstructed after 4 hours of running. The efficiency of the filter was considered to be "considerably below the requirements of this Department" and did not achieve the standard required of British armored vehicles.[409] According to British investigations, the Tiger was also very poorly suited for operation in mud. A report on comparative trials of British, American, Soviet, and captured German tanks in mud described the Tiger's performance simply as "very poor".[410] The Tiger was considered to be the worst performer out of all vehicles tested.[411] British post-war study of German tank development suggested that the official approach to dealing with mud was simply to avoid it.[412] Sensitivity to mud and dust in a theater with no shortage of either compounded the Tiger's technical issues and performed no small part in sapping the strength of Tiger battalions operating in Italy.

---

[408] Canadian Military Headquarters, London (CMHQ), Files Block No. 55 - 5776, Image 567

[409] Canadian Military Headquarters, London (CMHQ), Files Block No. 55 - 5773, Image 912

[410] Canadian Military Headquarters, London (CMHQ), Files Block No. 55 - 5777, Image 3829

[411] Fighting Vehicle Proving Establishment *Report No. F.T.1553 on Comparative Trials of Various A.F.V's in Soft Ground Conditions*

[412] Canadian Military Headquarters, London (CMHQ), Files Block No. 55 - 5777, Image 3916

British Tiger Hunters

As discovered in penetration trials, the 17-pounder gun was a viable weapon against the Tiger, capable of penetrating its armor at long range. This was not a surprise. Work on a powerful new anti-tank gun intended to tackle prospective enemy tanks began back in the summer of 1941.[413] The anti-tank performance of this gun was considered to be on par with the Tiger's 88 mm KwK 36.[414]

The powerful anti-tank gun came with a size and weight to match. While the British had the gun tractors to pull around a nearly three ton cannon,[415] it was difficult to find a tank or tank destroyer to put it in. It was proposed that the 17-pounder could be mounted in the turret of a TOG II tank, which was one of the vehicle's chief selling points.[416] After the Ministry of Supply dismissed the Special Vehicle Design Committee and shut down the project, a new chassis was required.[417] The Cromwell, Britain's latest cruiser tank, was chosen for this role. The project received the General Staff index A.30. The Cromwell chassis was lengthened to accommodate a new turret, one very similar in design to the TOG II. Even though the goal of this project was to quickly develop a tank destroyer using off-the-shelf parts, work progressed slowly. The first prototype was inspected by the Tank Board at Farnborough on August 13th, 1942; the second prototype was inspected at Lulworth on January 21st, 1943. At the time, rather than penetrating thick armor close up, the 17-pounder was expected to be used at extreme ranges against the Pz.Kpfw.IV Ausf.G. Both tanks were estimated to have an effective engagement range of 3000 yards (2743 m), at which distance the 17-pounder could penetrate the German tank's armor but the 7.5 cm KwK 40 L/43 could not penetrate the A.30 in return. Since the conclusion of fighting in North Africa was expected to bring an end to such long range tank duels, the

---

[413] CAB 63/166, *Design and production of heavy tanks*
[414] CAB 66/50/12, Select Committee on National Expenditure: *Report on Tank Production*
[415] Y. Pasholok, *Dlinnaya ruka po-angliyski*, https://warspot.ru/5976-dlinnaya-ruka-po-angliyski, retrieved on December 5th, 2023
[416] CAB 63/166, *Design and production of heavy tanks*
[417] P. Samsonov, *Landships Left in Port*, https://www.tankarchives.ca/2023/05/landships-left-in-port.html, retrieved on December 6th, 2023

value of this vehicle was limited. Nevertheless, the General Staff made the decision to order 200 units.[418]

TOG II, Bovington Tank Museum. This massive tank was Britain's only option for carrying the 17-pounder in 1941. It was never put into service, but its turret inspired the turret of the Challenger I with the same gun. *(Peter Samsonov)*

---

[418] D. Fletcher, *The Universal Tank*, HMSO, London, 1993, p.84

The number of tanks mounting these guns was soon revised. As of April 30th, 1943, General Staff policy called for 30% of tanks to carry the 17-pounder gun, 60% to carry a 75 mm gun, and the remaining 10% to carry a 95 mm howitzer. While the latter two weapons could fit in existing 6-pounder mountings, finding a chassis for the 17-pounder was more difficult. The A.30 would be available in small numbers and it was not clear when production could begin.[419]

Fortunately, new options revealed themselves. Work on fitting the 17-pounder into the turret of American Sherman tanks began in June of 1943.[420] This work resulted in the creation of the Sherman IC and Sherman VC tanks, unofficially nicknamed Firefly. The GMC M10 tank destroyer was also considered a suitable chassis. Vehicles with the new gun were most commonly designated 17-pdr M10 SP, with the names Achilles IC and Achilles IIC entering use close to the end of the war.

The decision to rearm American vehicles proved correct. The A.30 only entered production under the name Challenger I in March of 1944. Production proceeded at a lethargic pace, with only 34 units finished by the end of June and the 100-tank batch finished only by fall. To compare, by the end of June 1944 the British had 358 Sherman IC and VC tanks[421] and 124 Achilles tank destroyers with 17-pounder guns.[422]

---

[419] Canadian Military Headquarters, London (CMHQ), Files Block No. 55 - 5777, Image 4423-4424

[420] D. Fletcher, *The Universal Tank*, HMSO, London, 1993, p.85

[421] Y. Pasholok, *Bolshegoloviy kreyser*, https://warspot.ru/13021-bolshegolovyy-kreyser, retrieved on December 6th, 2023

[422] Tank AFVs, *17Pdr SP Achilles*, https://tank-afv.com/ww2/gb/17pdr-SP-Achilles.php, retrieved on February 20th, 2024

Sherman VC, colloquially known as the Firefly, Bovington Tank Museum. Conversion of American tanks was necessary to obtain sufficient numbers of vehicles to deal with heavy German armor in time for the Normandy campaign. *(Peter Samsonov)*

17-pounder M10 SP or Achilles IIC, Bovington Tank Museum. Even though the GMC M10 already had a powerful 3" gun, the British re-armed some of them with their own 17-pounder. *(Peter Samsonov)*

The Artillery branch chose another way to mechanize the 17-pounder. Valuing a low profile over high speed, Vickers was ordered to develop a chassis based on the Valentine tank in early 1943. The prototype presented on May 24th, 1943, was unconventional to say the least. In order to fit such a large gun on a very small platform, it had to be mounted backwards, with the barrel hanging above the engine deck. This solution also reduced the overhang of the gun and shortened the overall length of the vehicle. Despite many complaints, 800 tank destroyers designated 17-pdr Valentine SP were ordered in June of 1943. Like the tank destroyer converted from the GMC M10, the Valentine tank destroyer also received its own name towards the end of the war: Archer. The Archer ended up being much more numerous than the Challenger, with 200 units built by September of 1944.[423]

---

[423] Y. Pasholok, *SAU zadom napered*, https://warspot.ru/12075-sau-zadom-naperyod, retrieved on December 7th, 2023

17-pounder Valentine SP or Archer, Bovington Tank Museum. This vehicle had an unconventional layout and was found to be wanting in many ways, but still outnumbered the Challenger I more than three to one. *(Peter Samsonov)*

Even though the British already had an effective anti-tank gun to face Tiger tanks by the time the vehicle was discovered, it took quite some time until they themselves could field armored vehicles that could take out a Tiger tank at long range. Not only was there no rush to put such a vehicle out on the battlefield, the British began to move away from 6-pounder guns in their cruiser and infantry tanks, replacing them with general purpose 75 mm guns. While these guns had poorer performance against thick armor, they had a much more powerful high explosive round, which made them much more useful at the majority of the missions carried out by tanks in the Second World War. The discovery of a new heavily armored enemy tank did not cause a reversal of this policy. In the event that British tanks encountered heavy enemy armor, it was expected that the attached Firefly (in units armed with Sherman tanks) or Challenger (in units armed with Cromwell tanks) could take care of it while tanks with general purpose 75 mm guns could handle enemy medium tanks and infantry.[424]

---

[424] P. Samsonov, *A Firefly with a Stinger*, https://www.tankarchives.ca/2023/03/a-firefly-with-stinger.html, retrieved on December 7th, 2023

American Tiger Hunters

The Americans identified the need for a new powerful anti-tank gun around the same time as the British. Work on adapting the 3" model 1918 AA gun began in late 1940. Unlike the British, the Americans started thinking about mechanizing this weapon almost immediately. However, the American tank destroyer concept was a very different one. Rather than a fully or even semi-enclosed armored fighting vehicle, the 3" GMC T1 approved for development in January of 1941 consisted simply of the gun mounted atop a High Speed Tractor M2. Only a gun shield offered any protection for the crew. The vehicle had to deploy its spade before firing and could not fire on the move.[425] Procurement of 1580 units was authorized in January of 1942. The vehicle was standardized as the GMC M5.[426] Trials revealed many issues with the design and the project was canceled in August of the same year.[427]

A much more promising chassis was available than the light aircraft tractor: the Medium Tank M3. A vehicle designated GMC T24 mounting the same gun was developed. The gun was mounted on an armored chassis and could be brought to action much more quickly, but there was still little protection for the crew. Nevertheless, gunnery trials held in November 1941 proved that the chassis of the Medium Tank M3 was a suitable one for a 3" gun.[428] Development of a heavier and better armored tank destroyer was recommended. This project, designated GMC T35, was based on the chassis of the Medium Tank M4A2 and mounted the 3" Gun T12, a weapon with the same ballistics as the AA gun adapted for installation into the Heavy Tank T1. To keep weight down, the GMC T35 had thinner armor than the M4A2, no coaxial machine gun, and an open top. The GMC T35 and T35E1 prototypes arrived at the Aberdeen Proving Grounds in April and demonstrated on May 2nd, 1942. The T35E1 was standardized as the GMC M10. The GMC M10 could be produced rapidly as very few changes were made to the chassis of the base medium tank. 105

---

[425] N. Moran, *Can Openers*, Echo Point Books & Media, Brattleboro Vermont, 2017. pp.100-101

[426] N. Moran, *Can Openers*, Echo Point Books & Media, Brattleboro Vermont, 2017. pp.102

[427] N. Moran, *Can Openers*, Echo Point Books & Media, Brattleboro Vermont, 2017. pp.109

[428] N. Moran, *Can Openers*, Echo Point Books & Media, Brattleboro Vermont, 2017. pp.110-111

vehicles were ready by September 30th, 1942, and the vehicle saw battle in North Africa by the end of the year.[429] Rates of production were incredibly high with 2190 GMC M10 built at Fisher Tank Division and 711 GMC M10A1 (M10 with a Ford GAA engine) at Ford just during the first half of 1943. In total, Ford built 1038 GMC M10A1 by the end of 1943. Fisher built 375 GMC M10A1, 4993 GMC M10, and 300 additional chassis that were later completed as the GMC M36. By the end of 1943, the US Army had over 6000 tank destroyers capable of defeating the Tiger tank at long range.[430]

GMC M10, Overlord Museum. The 3" gun used on this tank destroyer was capable of penetrating the front of a Tiger tank at long range and was already in the field when the Tiger tank was discovered. *(Peter Samsonov)*

Despite the same caliber as the Soviet 76 mm F-34 and British 17-pounder, the performance of these three guns was very different. The American 3" gun

---

[429] N. Moran, *Can Openers*, Echo Point Books & Media, Brattleboro Vermont, 2017. pp.122-130

[430] Y. Pasholok, *Sredniy istrebitel' po-amerikanski*, https://warspot.ru/16063-sredniy-istrebitel-po-amerikanski, retrieved on December 7th, 2023

was a much more powerful weapon than the Soviet gun with a heavier APCBC shell weighing 14.89 lbs (6.75 kg) fired at 2600 f/s (792 m/s). According to American data, this translated into penetration of 5.95" (151 mm) of homogeneous armor sloped at 20 degrees at point-blank range. At 1500 yards (1371 m) the gun could still penetrate 4.1" (104 cm) of armor, making it an effective weapon against the Tiger.[431]

It is worth noting that the Americans did not stop here and development of a tank destroyer with a 90 mm gun based on the 90 mm AA Gun M1 was proposed to the Ordnance Committee as early as April 17th, 1942. This work resulted in the GMC M36 family of tank destroyers. New turrets carrying 90 mm guns were installed on the chassis of the GMC M10, GMC M10A1, and Medium Tank M4A3 to give 1400 tank destroyers by the end of 1944 with guns that could combat not just the Tiger but also the much better armored Panther and Tiger II. 2324 GMC M36 were converted in total.[432]

It is often said that the Americans intentionally under-gunned their tanks, relying on tank destroyers to tackle enemy tanks instead. This is not the case. In fact, in response to the very earliest work on a tank destroyer armed with a 3" gun, the Chief of Infantry wrote an objection, stating that "the best antitank weapon is the tank". American tank destroyers were relatively lightly armored and relied on speed and surprise to defeat enemy tank spearheads. They lacked the offensive power that was granted to a tank by its thick armor. Therefore, development of tank guns aimed to match weapons used by tank destroyers.[433]

The 3" Gun T12 was taken as the basis for a new tank gun. The new weapon was called 76 mm Gun T1 and later standardized as the 76 mm Gun M1. Trials showed that the gun could fit into the turret of a Sherman tank and early trials showed promising results. On August 17th, 1942, the Armor Board recommended that the Medium Tank M4A1 (76 M1) be declared a substitute

---

[431] Canadian Military Headquarters, London (CMHQ), Files Block No. 55 - 5788, Image 3419
[432] P. Samsonov, *Amerikanskiy Zveroboy*, https://warspot.ru/19927-amerikanskiy-zveroboy, retrieved on December 7th, 2023
[433] N. Moran, *Can Openers*, Echo Point Books & Media, Brattleboro Vermont, 2017. p.100

standard and 1000 units ordered.[434] This was a premature move, as there were considerable issues with the sights and controls of the gun. The order of 1000 was cut to just 12. This didn't mean that the Americans gave up on mounting a 76 mm gun in a Sherman tank and by May of 1943 there was already discussion of using the turret developed for the Medium Tank T23 with an improved 76 mm gun on the chassis of a Sherman tank.[435] This time, the gun proved much more usable. Despite the excitement over its performance, the Armor Board was vocally against stopping production of tanks armed with 75 mm gun, stating the desired ratio of 76 mm guns to 75 mm guns as 1:2 (one platoon in each company) particularly due to the superior HE performance of the lower velocity 75 mm gun.[436]

---

[434] Canadian Military Headquarters, London (1939-1947) - 17473, Image 71
[435] Canadian Military Headquarters, London (CMHQ), Files Block No. 55 - 5778, Image 4399
[436] Canadian Military Headquarters, London (CMHQ), Files Block No. 55 - 5774, Image 4162-4163

Medium Tank M4A1(76)W, Overlord Museum. These tanks armed with a powerful 76 mm gun that could penetrate the Tiger's front armor arrived in time to take part of the Normandy invasion, but were intentionally held back from the initial landings as it was believed that German heavy tanks were not available in large enough numbers to justify deploying a new type of tank. *(Peter Samsonov)*

Despite this enthusiasm for production of the Medium Tank M4 armed with a 76 mm gun, there was less of a rush to issue them. The first 130 M4A1(76)W tanks arrived in Britain on April 10th, 1944. None were issued to the force being prepared for landings in Normandy. The new gun came with its share of drawbacks, including the need to train troops on the new equipment and complications arising from the use of a different caliber of ammunition. It was felt that this was too high of a price to pay for increased penetration, as the 75 mm gun was sufficient to handle the Pz.Kpfw.IV medium tank and the Tiger had been encountered in such small numbers in Tunisia and Sicily that they would be easily handled by tank destroyers. The Americans were aware of the Panther due to reports from the USSR and had even captured tanks of this type in Italy, but it was thought that this tank, like the Tiger, would be employed in small numbers and only as a part of specialized battalions. As a result, no tanks with 76 mm guns landed in France on D-Day.[437] This was a grave mistake as the heavier Panther tank was nearly as common as the lighter Pz.Kpfw.IV. The authorized strength of German tank division in 1944 was 73 Panther tanks and 78 Pz.Kpfw.IV tanks.[438] In practice, this figure was slightly lower, but the proportion of Panthers to older tank models in France reached 46% in June of 1944.[439] This shortfall in Allied firepower was quickly remedied after the first weeks of fighting, however the primary cause of this was the presence of an unexpectedly large number of Panther tanks, rather than Tigers.[440]

Heavy Tank T26E3, Bovington Tank Museum. This tank was built as a response to the Tiger, with a gun that could defeat the armor of the German heavy tank at long range where it could not be penetrated in return. *(Peter Samsonov)*

---

[437] S.J. Zaloga, *M4 (76mm) Sherman Medium Tank 1943-65*, Osprey Publishing, Oxford, 2003. Kindle Edition, pp.25-34

[438] B. Kast, Die Organisation der Panzerdivisionen 1939 und 1944 – Quantitative Analyse, in: *Achtung Panzer? Zur Panzerwaffe der Wehrmacht*. Military History Group, 2022, pp. 124-125

[439] S.J. Zaloga, *M4 (76mm) Sherman Medium Tank 1943-65*, Osprey Publishing, Oxford, 2003. Kindle Edition, p.32

[440] S.J. Zaloga, *M4 (76mm) Sherman Medium Tank 1943-65*, Osprey Publishing, Oxford, 2003. Kindle Edition, pp.35-37

That is not to say the Americans dismissed the Tiger completely until the landings at Normandy. A need was recognized for a heavy tank with a powerful gun that could knock out a Tiger or Panther at long range and enough armor that the enemy couldn't do the same.[441] In fact, the purpose of the Medium Tank T26 was explicitly described as "to provide an improved tank with armor equivalent or superior to the German Mk VI and armed with 90 mm Gun" as early as April of 1943.[442] Characteristics of the Medium Tank T26 were also compared against those of the Tiger in a July 1943 A.F.V. Situation Report.[443] General Gladeon Barnes, a key figure in American tank development, described the T26 as having about the same effective armor as a Tiger with a slightly better gun at a much lower weight.[444] The T26 project led to the Medium Tank T26E1 (later reclassified as a heavy) and eventually the Heavy Tank T26E3, which was standardized as the Heavy Tank M26 in 1945. Only 20 T26E3 tanks made it to Europe in time to see battle before VE Day, making it much less common than tank destroyers armed with the same 90 mm gun.[445]

As this sequence of events shows, the Americans were ready for the arrival of the Tiger tank. GMC M10 tank destroyers with 3" guns capable of penetrating it from long range were already in the field by the time Tiger tanks were first encountered, and development of a new more powerful 90 mm gun began before the Tiger reached the battlefield. Where the Americans did not keep up was armor. It was therefore not possible for either tank destroyers armed with 90 mm guns or medium tanks armed with 76 mm guns to fight the Tiger tank at a range where they were immune to return fire.

---

[441] Canadian Military Headquarters, London (CMHQ), Files Block No. 55 - 5772, Image 4044

[442] Canadian Military Headquarters, London (CMHQ), Files Block No. 55 - 5778, Image 4263

[443] Canadian Military Headquarters, London (CMHQ), Files Block No. 55 - 5774, Image 3704

[444] Canadian Military Headquarters, London (CMHQ), Files Block No. 55 - 5779, Image 57

[445] P. Samsonov, *Americanskaya zebra protiv nemetskikh tigrov i panter*, https://warspot.ru/18019-amerikanskaya-zebra-protiv-nemetskih-tigrov-i-panter, retrieved on December 11th, 2023

The Tiger's Last Bow

In preparation of the landings in Europe, a comprehensive guide on combating Tiger tanks was put together by the British School of Tank Technology. The report gave only approximate figures, as it was noted that the quality of German armor varied wildly.[446] The figures provided in the report were based on the performance of British machinable quality plate.[447] Even this data gives us a good indication of how guns of the Western Allies expected to perform against a threat the British already had a year to study.

A 17-pounder gun firing APCBC shot performed much better than the AP shot first tested in Tunisia. The turret front and driver's visor plate could be defeated at ranges of up to 2000 yards (1829 m) at an angle of 30 degrees. The distance at which it could be penetrated at normal is so great that it is not shown in the diagram, but it is well in excess of 3000 yards (2743 m). The turret side and hull superstructure were likewise vulnerable at great range, up to 2000 yards (1829 m) at an angle of 40 degrees and much longer ranges at normal.[448]

The 6-pounder gun firing APCBC could be expected to penetrate at much shorter ranges. The front was considered vulnerable at a range of 450 yards (411 m) or less at normal. At an angle of 20 degrees, it could only be penetrated at point-blank range. The side was vulnerable at ranges of up to 1500 yards (1371 m) at normal, 500 yards (457 m) at 30 degrees, and at point-blank range at 40 degrees.[449]

The American 3" gun was also evaluated. It was expected to penetrate the front of a Tiger from a range of 1200 yards (1097 m) at normal or 500 yards (457 m) at an angle of 25 degrees. At an angle of 30 degrees, penetration even at point-blank range was considered unlikely. The side was vulnerable at ranges

---

[446] School of Tank Technology, *Attack on German Panther & Tiger Tanks*, p.9
[447] School of Tank Technology, *Attack on German Panther & Tiger Tanks*, p.1
[448] School of Tank Technology, *Attack on German Panther & Tiger Tanks*, p.22
[449] School of Tank Technology, *Attack on German Panther & Tiger Tanks*, p.28

of up to 2500 yards (2286 m) at normal, 1400 yards (1280 m) at an angle of 30 degrees, and at point-blank range at 40 degrees.[450]

The American and British 75 mm guns had no hope of penetrating the tank from the front. The sides were vulnerable at a range of up to 700 yards (640 m) at normal, 500 yards (457 m) at 10 degrees, 250 yards (228 m) at 20 degrees, and impenetrable at 30 degrees. The rear could also be penetrated at a range of 500 yards (457 m) at normal with the effective range likewise dropping rapidly at greater angles.[451] Like the British 2-pounder or Soviet 45 mm anti-tank gun, the American 37 mm wasn't entirely hopeless when facing the Tiger, but close to it. The turret and superstructure side could be penetrated at 400 yards (365 m) with APCBC shot. The lower hull armor behind the road wheels could be penetrated at a range of 1300 yards (1188 m) at normal or 500 yards (457 m) at a 30 degree angle. The manual notes that this was not an easy shot to make.[452]

The Americans released their own series of penetration diagrams on July 19th, 1944. Curiously, the data is only given for an angle of attack of 25 degrees, making it difficult to compare with data obtained by other nations. At this angle, only the 90 mm gun had a chance of penetrating the front armor. The driver's visor plate was vulnerable at ranges of up to 1200 yards (1097 m). The lower hull and turret front were immune. The upper side of the hull as well as the sides and rear of the turret were vulnerable to attack at a range of 2680 yards (2451 m). The side was also vulnerable to the 3" and 76 mm guns at a range of 720 yards (656 m) and the 57 mm Gun M1 (a copy of the British 6-pounder Mk.I) at 240 yards (219 m). The same weapons were also effective when attacking the rear hull armor at ranges of 2600, 550, and 170 yards respectively (2377, 503, and 155 meters).[453]

The manual also supplied some photographs from penetration trials of a Tiger tank. 57 mm shot fired at the 3.22" (81.8 mm) thick turret armor at a range of 1200 yards (1097 m) at normal penetrated the armor, knocking out a petal.

---

[450] School of Tank Technology, *Attack on German Panther & Tiger Tanks*, p.34
[451] School of Tank Technology, *Attack on German Panther & Tiger Tanks*, p.40
[452] School of Tank Technology, *Attack on German Panther & Tiger Tanks*, p.46
[453] Office of the Chief of Ordnance, *Vulnerability Tests of German Tanks Pz Kw III, Pz Kw IV, Pz Kw VI, 19 July 1944*, pp.28-30

Attack on the upper side hull of the same thickness with a 3" shell from a range of 2530 yards (2313 m) at normal made a 62 inch by 27 inch (157 by 69 cm) breach in the side of the hull. Attack on the rear hull with the same shell from 3740 yards (3420 m) at normal did not shatter the plate, but still achieved a jagged penetration 6 inches (152 mm) in diameter. Attack on the 4.05" (103 mm) thick front hull at ranges from 810 to 1640 yards (740-1500 m) resulted in penetration with severe spalling and cracking of the plate.[454]

The 90 mm gun proved an even more powerful weapon. Two shots at the 4.21" (107 mm) thick lower front hull made at 30 degrees from 1210 and 1740 yards (1106 and 1591 m) both penetrated the armor. The same component on a different Tiger tank measuring just 4.05" (103 mm) shattered after being hit four times at normal from ranges of 2820 to 4090 yards (2579-3740 m). 90 mm APC shells remained effective even at high angles of attack. The 2.49" (63 mm) lower side armor could be penetrated at an angle of 55 degrees from a range of 400 yards (365 m), leaving behind a jagged hole. Both the 76 and 90 mm guns were clearly very effective against the armor of the German heavy tank.[455]

Updated penetration diagrams were released by January of 1945.[456] All figures were now given at normal, making them easier to compare with British findings. The 3" and 76 mm guns were expected to penetrate the front hull of a Tiger tank at the same range of 1200 yards as the British document, but the penetration was against the more highly sloped lower front as opposed to the almost vertical driver's visor plate. The front of the turret was expected to be penetrated at a range of up to 1600 yards (1463 m) at normal. The penetration range against the upper side was estimated at 2600 yards (2377 m), just 100 yards longer than the British expected.

The range evaluated for the 75 mm gun was instead shorter, 500 yards (457 m). Likewise, no success was expected against the front hull. Figures for the 37

---

[454] Office of the Chief of Ordnance, *Vulnerability Tests of German Tanks Pz Kw III, Pz Kw IV, Pz Kw VI, 19 July 1944*, pp.31-32

[455] Office of the Chief of Ordnance, *Vulnerability Tests of German Tanks Pz Kw III, Pz Kw IV, Pz Kw VI, 19 July 1944*, pp.33-34

[456] ETO Technical Intelligence Report No.114, *Vulnerability Charts of German Tanks*

mm gun were also less optimistic: 100 yards (91 m) against the upper side and 800 yards (731 m) against the lower.

The star of this pamphlet was the new 90 mm gun, which was capable of penetrating the front of the turret from 3000 yards (2743 m) and the tougher sloped front hull at 2600 yards (2377 m). The side could be penetrated from 4300 yards (3932 m).

Specifics of how Tiger tanks were being used in the field were still discovered. A series of questions was presented to German POWs with knowledge of tank units. The British were clearly interested in whether or not the reliability issues identified in Italy had been corrected. The questionnaire led with questions of a technical nature: what percentage of tanks were in workshops for reasons of mechanical breakdown, why, and for how long. Not enough data was gathered for a definitive rate of availability to be determined, but one POW estimated that on average 2 tanks out of his company of 14 were always out of action. Tanks usually spent 2-3 days in a battalion workshop if sufficient parts were available. It was also noted that, with the exception of one POW (a general), no one considered the existing supply of spare parts to be sufficient.[457] The Tiger still suffered from engine defects and issues with track pins working themselves loose.[458]

The British were interested in Tiger tactics as well, as they were liable to be different in this theater than in the close quarters and difficult terrain encountered in Italy. In North-Western Europe, Tigers were employed in 4-tank platoons. Tankers were taught platoon and company tactics and were instructed never to operate vehicles alone, although this could happen in Normandy depending on the circumstances.[459]

---

[457] Canadian Military Headquarters, London (CMHQ), Files Block No. 55 - 5777, Image 2320

[458] Canadian Military Headquarters, London (CMHQ), Files Block No. 55 - 5777, Image 2321

[459] Canadian Military Headquarters, London (CMHQ), Files Block No. 55 - 5777, Image 2323

Based on inspection of captured Tigers, the British concluded that the maneuverability of such a large and heavy tank would be reduced compared to a medium tank. While POWs admitted that the maneuverability of the Tiger was less than that of the Panther, it was never found to be an issue. The British also tried to validate their hypothesis that the slow turret traverse made engaging targets difficult, but no useful evidence was found one way or the other.[460]

As with the Red Army, field penetration trials were conducted with Tiger tanks as targets. In part, a Tiger tank was found near Mook and chosen as a target for 105 mm M67 HEAT shells. This Tiger had no battle damage or even identifiable mechanical damage, and it was likely abandoned after running out of fuel. The enemy stripped the tank of all ammunition and internal fittings that could be removed before abandoning it. Firing was performed at a range of 150 yards (137 m) as the terrain made it impossible to fire at the tank from a longer range.

The trials showed that 105 mm HEAT had no issues with penetrating even the toughest armor of the Tiger. The first four shots were aimed at the nose plate (102 mm at 25 degrees), which was penetrated every time at angles of impact of up to 20 degrees. The fifth shot penetrated the gun mantlet, breaking and dislodging four bolts holding the gun cradle. The sixth shot hit the edge of the gun mantlet, not penetrating into the tank but gouging it to such a degree that would restrict the elevation of the gun. Two more shots were fired at the side of the turret and turret at a high angle (65-80 degrees from normal), none of which were effective. The ninth and final shot hit the gun mantlet again, penetrating it completely and splitting the hull roof above the bow gunner's position. This damage was described as "far in excess of what could normally be expected". It was concluded that any part of the Tiger could be penetrated by the M67 shell, with the possible exception of some parts of the armor. The trials doubled as a demonstration of the shell to men of the 2nd Canadian Armored Brigade, who were all encouraged by the performance of the new equipment and felt confident in taking on Tiger and Panther tanks with it.[461]

---

[460] Canadian Military Headquarters, London (CMHQ), Files Block No. 55 - 5777, Image 2323

[461] Canadian Military Headquarters, London (CMHQ), Files Block No. 55 - 5777, Image 1683

Penetration Trials at the End of the War

Even though the Tiger was long out of production by 1945 and the British were aware of German AFVs with thicker armor and more powerful guns, the Tiger nevertheless presented an interest. Two Tiger tanks (turret numbers 114 and 334) captured in Normandy were transported to the UK for testing. Tiger 114 was used for survivability trials at the Shoeburyness range, but no details of these trials are available.[462]

Tiger 334 was also subjected to trials. Thorough firing trials were held at Shoeburyness on March 7th-22nd, 1945[463] with supplementary trials conducted on April 23-27th, 1945.[464] A large spectrum of infantry weapons, towed guns, and tank guns was used in this trial, including some that were not available when Tiger tanks were shot up in Tunisia.[465]

Attack with rifle caliber ammunition showed that the Tiger was vulnerable to splash. It was possible to wound crew members by firing at the end of the gun mantlet or at the turret escape hatch with .303" ball ammunition. Armor piercing .303" bullets could jam the hull machine gun ball and driver's visor. It was also possible for fragments of the bullets to enter the turret ring, but this type of attack was unlikely to jam the turret.[466] Firing from above, a rifleman could penetrate the seal around the driver's hatch or damage the tank's radiators.[467]

---

[462] B.O. Newsome, *The Tiger Tank and Allied Intelligence Volume III, Tiger 131: From Africa to Europe*, Tank Archives Press, Coronado, 2020, pp.143-144
[463] DTD Experimental Report AT No.252 armor Branch *Report On Firing Trial against German Tiger Pz.Kw.VI Parts I-IV*, p.1
[464] DTD Experimental Report AT No.252 armor Branch *Report On Firing Trial against German Tiger Pz.Kw.VI Part III and Part IV*
[465] DTD Experimental Report AT No.252 armor Branch *Report On Firing Trial against German Tiger Pz.Kw.VI Parts I-IV*, p.1
[466] DTD Experimental Report AT No.252 armor Branch *Report On Firing Trial against German Tiger Pz.Kw.VI Part I*, p.4
[467] DTD Experimental Report AT No.252 armor Branch *Report On Firing Trial against German Tiger Pz.Kw.VI Part I*, p.2

Performance of airburst HE was simulated by firing a 25-pounder gun-howitzer against wooden boards suspended above the tank. Trials showed that the tank was very vulnerable to this kind of attack. The first round fired caused severe leakage to the water radiator. The testers estimated that the loss of water would be sufficient for the engine to overheat within five minutes.[468] The radiators could also be severely damaged by 20 mm AP and incendiary ammunition fired from a Hispano autocannon mounted on aircraft.[469]

A 6-pounder gun was used in these trials, firing APDS ammunition unlike earlier trials that only used AP. Aiming at the lower front plate (102 mm at 24 degrees) the gun was expected to penetrate from a range of 1000 yards (914 m). This tank was missing track links commonly carried on the front. A section of Panther track was mounted to simulate it. Penetrating this part of the hull was much harder when it was covered with track links, and the testers estimated that the main armor would only be defeated at very close range.[470] The track link was also found to be an effective means of protecting the side of the turret from 6-pdr APDS. A penetration was achieved at an angle of 40 degrees and a velocity representing the range of 1200 yards (1097 m), but at the same angle negligible damage was caused even at a velocity representing close range attack when track links were mounted. Three rounds were also fired at the gun mantlet (100 mm thick) at 30 degrees from normal. The estimated limit of penetration suggested an effective range of about 1200 yards (1097 m) with this kind of attack.[471]

6-pounder APCBC was also used in this trial, which was also not available when the Tiger was tested in Tunisia. APCBC was not fired at the front of the hull. The first target was the side of the turret, which the shot penetrated at an angle of 20 degrees and a velocity equivalent to about 500 yards (457 m). At 30

---

[468] DTD Experimental Report AT No.252 armor Branch *Report On Firing Trial against German Tiger Pz.Kw.VI Part I*, p.2-3
[469] DTD Experimental Report AT No.252 armor Branch *Report On Firing Trial against German Tiger Pz.Kw.VI Part I*, p.4
[470] DTD Experimental Report AT No.252 armor Branch *Report On Firing Trial against German Tiger Pz.Kw.VI Part II*, p.2
[471] DTD Experimental Report AT No.252 armor Branch *Report On Firing Trial against German Tiger Pz.Kw.VI Part II*, p.5

degrees, the shot did not penetrate.[472] The upper side performed the same. A shot at 30 degrees fired at a similar velocity failed to penetrate, while a shot at 20 degrees penetrated the tank and likely would have killed the driver with the fragments of the armor.[473] The report concludes that a penetration of the side of the turret or hull could be expected at a range of 1350 yards (1234 m) at an angle of 20 degrees.[474] A shot at the lower side (62 mm thick) at a velocity corresponding to a range of over 500 yards at an angle of 30 degrees penetrated the side, hitting the fuel tank and starting a fire. The report notes that such a shot was only possible due to a missing wheel and would have been difficult otherwise.[475]

6-pounder APCBC shot was also fired at the front of the turret. The shot hit 1.5 inches (38 mm) above the bottom of the gun mantlet and deflected downwards, making a 7.5x4 inch (190x102 mm) hole in the roof of the driver's compartment. Fragments of the shot and the roof tore up the dummy representing the driver and inflicted considerable damage on the gearbox. Other members of the crew may also have been struck by the shards.[476]

As with the 6-pounder, the 17-pounder used in this trial had new ammunition: APDS and APCBC. APDS shot fired at the side of the turret failed to penetrate at a velocity corresponding to a range of about 1000 yards (914 m) at an angle of 50 degrees, but penetrated at 40 degrees from normal. A round with a velocity corresponding to a range of about 2000 yards penetrated the side at 36 degrees. It was estimated that at 40 degrees from normal, penetration could be achieved at a range of up to 1300 yards (1280 m).[477] The side of the hull turned out to be much weaker than the turret, penetrated at an angle of 50

---

[472] DTD Experimental Report AT No.252 armor Branch *Report On Firing Trial against German Tiger Pz.Kw.VI Part II*, p.3
[473] DTD Experimental Report AT No.252 armor Branch *Report On Firing Trial against German Tiger Pz.Kw.VI Part II*, p.4
[474] DTD Experimental Report AT No.252 armor Branch *Report On Firing Trial against German Tiger Pz.Kw.VI Part III*, p.1
[475] DTD Experimental Report AT No.252 armor Branch *Report On Firing Trial against German Tiger Pz.Kw.VI Part II*, p.4
[476] DTD Experimental Report AT No.252 armor Branch *Report On Firing Trial against German Tiger Pz.Kw.VI Part II*, p.3-4
[477] DTD Experimental Report AT No.252 armor Branch *Report On Firing Trial against German Tiger Pz.Kw.VI Part II*, p.4

degrees from normal and a velocity corresponding to a range of almost 2000 yards (1829 m) even though the hardness of the plate was identical. Damage to the inside was severe and such a penetration on a fully stowed Tiger would likely have resulted in an ammunition fire.[478] APDS shot performed similarly well against the upper front hull (102 mm at 10 degrees). A penetration was expected when firing at 41 degrees from normal at a range under 800 yards.[479] Even the gun mantlet was not a serious obstacle for 17-pounder APDS shot. A reinforced portion of the mantlet was penetrated at an angle of 40 degrees and a velocity corresponding to a range of over 1000 yards (914 m). It was estimated that this armor could be defeated from a range of up to 1500 yards (1372 m).[480]

17-pounder APCBC was also no slouch. At normal, the upper front hull plate (102 mm at 10 degrees) was penetrated twice at a velocity corresponding to a range of well over 2000 yards. It was estimated that this part of the armor was vulnerable at any fighting range. The Tiger's upper front hull could be penetrated by 17-pounder APCBC at angles of up to 41 degrees from normal, although at that sharp of an angle the gun would have to be at near point-blank range. Defeat of the lower front hull (102 mm at 24 degrees) was also considered likely at any range.[481] Penetration of the upper side of the hull was expected at ranges of under 900 yards (823 m) at an angle of 45 degrees. The same armor could be penetrated at 50 degrees from normal only at near point-blank range.[482]

The final tank gun to take part in the trials was the Sherman's 75 mm M3 firing M61 APCBC shells as used in previous trials. The upper hull side (82 mm) could not be defeated when hit at an angle of 20 degrees. However, the lower side (63 mm) was penetrated at full service charge from a range of 150 feet (45 m).[483]

---

[478] DTD Experimental Report AT No.252 armor Branch *Report On Firing Trial against German Tiger Pz.Kw.VI Part II*, p.5

[479] DTD Experimental Report AT No.252 armor Branch *Report On Firing Trial against German Tiger Pz.Kw.VI Part II*, p.4

[480] DTD Experimental Report AT No.252 armor Branch *Report On Firing Trial against German Tiger Pz.Kw.VI Part II*, p.6

[481] DTD Experimental Report AT No.252 armor Branch *Report On Firing Trial against German Tiger Pz.Kw.VI Part II*, p.5

[482] DTD Experimental Report AT No.252 armor Branch *Report On Firing Trial against German Tiger Pz.Kw.VI Part III*, p.1

[483] DTD Experimental Report AT No.252 armor Branch *Report On Firing Trial against German Tiger Pz.Kw.VI Part II*, p.5

The remaining shots were fired using HE shells. A shell that hit the bottom of the gun mantlet extended cracks in the roof made by previous shots and introduced a new crack, although it's doubtful that such an effect could have been made if the roof was intact. Attack on the upper front hull only slightly damaged the weld seam. Attack on the rear of the turret was also ineffective, although fragments of the shell struck the radiators. The best place to aim with 75 mm HE was clearly the lower hull side. A shot that hit just 1 inch below the pannier floor destroyed the track, sheared the pannier floor, and dealt severe damage to the ammunition racks above it. If the Tiger was fully stowed, this shot would have likely resulted in an ammunition fire.[484] 25-pounder HE fired at the front and rear of the Tiger had similarly slight effect, but the shot at the side was not repeated with the larger gun.[485]

Infantry weapons were also put to the test. A PIAT proved capable of defeating any part of the Tiger's armor, including the lower front (102 mm at 24 degrees). The Tiger's wheels at least offered some protection for the lower sides, as if the projectile struck the wheels the HEAT jet would not have enough energy to penetrate the main armor.[486]

No.75 Hawkins anti-tank grenades statically detonated against the hull and turret roof caused significant cracking of the armor, although this was unlikely to harm the crew. Damage was likely to be caused by rivets holding on the hatch mountings dislodging as a result of the blast.[487] Large bundles of grenades could also damage the suspension and running gear. Ten No.75 Hawkins grenades (two rows of five) severed the track, destroying the axle of one bogie and the suspension assembly of another. A charge of fifteen grenades (box of twelve with three more placed on top) tore off three bogies and their suspension

---

[484] DTD Experimental Report AT No.252 armor Branch *Report On Firing Trial against German Tiger Pz.Kw.VI Part II*, p.5-6
[485] DTD Experimental Report AT No.252 armor Branch *Report On Firing Trial against German Tiger Pz.Kw.VI Part II*, p.6
[486] DTD Experimental Report AT No.252 armor Branch *Report On Firing Trial against German Tiger Pz.Kw.VI Part II*, p.7
[487] DTD Experimental Report AT No.252 armor Branch *Report On Firing Trial against German Tiger Pz.Kw.VI Part III*, p.2-3

assemblies. The pannier floor above the explosion split, but the hull floor plate held with only some bulging and surface pitting.[488]

The Tiger proved to be much more effectively protected against mines. A Mark V AT mine detonated underneath the track only dealt slight damage to the track links and wheels, and only two mines stacked on top of each other detonated in the middle of the track gave good results.[489] A pair of mines detonated on the inner side of the track also severed the bogie axles.[490]

Not surprisingly, it was concluded that the Tiger was vulnerable to a wide range of British anti-tank weapons. Penetration of the fighting compartment would likely have resulted in devastating damage due to the large amount of ammunition stored in the open. Projectiles hitting the lower portion of the gun mantlet deflected downwards into the thin and especially brittle roof armor, although the report notes that this trick was more difficult to pull off against the Tiger than the Panther owing to the former's lack of downward curve on the mantlet. Unlike other German tanks tested around the same time, this Tiger's armor did not prove liable to crack or flake under fire. Examination of the 60 and 80 mm plates showed that they were considerably softer than what was expected of German armor based on analysis of captured vehicles. It was theorized that the Germans began to produce softer armor in order to resolve the common issue with brittleness experienced by German tanks.[491] The report notes that the softer German armor behaved in a manner similar to British I.T.80E plate, with the exception of the brittle roof armor.[492]

---

[488] DTD Experimental Report AT No.252 armor Branch *Report On Firing Trial against German Tiger Pz.Kw.VI Part IV*, p.1-2

[489] DTD Experimental Report AT No.252 armor Branch *Report On Firing Trial against German Tiger Pz.Kw.VI Part II*, p.7-8

[490] DTD Experimental Report AT No.252 armor Branch *Report On Firing Trial against German Tiger Pz.Kw.VI Part IV*, p.1

[491] DTD Experimental Report AT No.252 armor Branch *Report On Firing Trial against German Tiger Pz.Kw.VI Part II*, p.8-10

[492] DTD Experimental Report AT No.252 armor Branch *Report On Firing Trial against German Tiger Pz.Kw.VI Parts I-IV Part III*, p.2

Motion Studies

The British did not limit themselves to the brief study of crew conditions in Tiger 131 conducted shortly after its capture in 1943. A detailed study of crew conditions in German tanks was carried out by Captain C. Turncliffe of the Motion Study Wing in 1947. Turncliffe studied the workspaces and controls available to crewmen of the Tiger, Panther, and Tiger II.[493]

The commander's position was criticized similarly to its evaluation in 1943. The commander had three positions in which he could perform his duties: sitting in the upper seat with his head looking out of the cupola, sitting on the lower seat, and standing on the rotating floor of the turret compartment. While the upper seat was comfortable on its own, no backrest was provided. The commander's back pressed uncomfortably against the gas mask case stowed behind him. This discomfort would no doubt increase if the vehicle was in motion. The commander was also cramped by the gun shield on the right and the turret wall on the left.[494]

The lower seat was more comfortable, as the upper seat folded down and served as a backrest. The width of the commander's station did not increase in this position. His workspace was still severely limited by the gun shield on the right. This time, the turret traverse gearbox chafed against the commander's leg on the left. Nevertheless, this was considered to be more comfortable than the upper position.[495]

The commander could also stand on the floor, but the proximity of the gun and turret traverse gearbox still made this position very cramped. There was nothing to hold on to; it was considered that he would be thrown against the folded seats behind him and the gearbox to his left if the tank was in motion.[496]

---

[493] WO 291/1003, *Motion Studies of German Tanks*, Section 1
[494] WO 291/1003, *Motion Studies of German Tanks*, Section 2, p.1
[495] WO 291/1003, *Motion Studies of German Tanks*, Section 2, p.1
[496] WO 291/1003, *Motion Studies of German Tanks*, Section 2, p.1

Generally, the commander's position was deemed "cramped and uncomfortable".[497]

The commander had an auxiliary handwheel, with which he could help the gunner traverse the turret. This feature was considered "basically sound but badly positioned".[498] The commander had to awkwardly twist his hand in order to operate it. In the upper position, his wrist also chafed against the cupola locking rod. The commander could not use this control on his own, as it needed to be unlocked by a latch on the gunner's handwheel. This was an issue, since the wheels were geared differently, and if the commander rotated his handwheel too quickly, the gunner's handwheel would slip out of his hand and the safety latch would re-engage.[499]

Criticism of the commander's vision devices was largely the same as in 1943. The cupola with five vision slits did not cover the entire 360 degrees around the tank and it was awkward to turn around in the commander's limited space to use the two slits pointing backwards when seated. There was also a provision for a binocular periscope that would allow the commander to correct his tank's fire without sticking his head out of the turret, but such a periscope was not fitted on this tank.[500] The fact that the flaps of the turret hatch stuck up vertically and increased the overall height of the tank when open was also criticized, as was the fact that the deep cupola restricted the commander's entrance and exit through the hatch.[501] The commander's vision equipment was described as "reasonable, but not fully adequate".[502]

Unlike the commander, the gunner's seat was not adjustable, but it had a backrest. Just as with the commander, while the seat was comfortable to sit on, the position was very cramped to work in. The rocking plate that controlled the power traverse was located very close to his seat, as a result of which he had to sit with his knees sharply bent. The position of the leg shield also required the

---

[497] WO 291/1003, *Motion Studies of German Tanks*, Section 2, p.1
[498] WO 291/1003, *Motion Studies of German Tanks*, Section 2, p.2
[499] WO 291/1003, *Motion Studies of German Tanks*, Section 2, p.1
[500] WO 291/1003, *Motion Studies of German Tanks*, Section 2, p.2
[501] WO 291/1003, *Motion Studies of German Tanks*, Section 2, p.6
[502] WO 291/1003, *Motion Studies of German Tanks*, Section 2, p.2

gunner to tilt his knees to the right, where they knocked against the elevation handwheel. If the gunner needed to lean forward, he had to twist his body further, increasing discomfort.[503]

The elevation handwheel was located to the right of the gunner and operated with his right hand. The handle of the wheel was too small to grip it with the whole hand, which made it difficult to use.[504] The trigger for the main gun was located on the shaft of the elevation handwheel, meaning that the gunner had to let go of the wheel in order to fire it.[505]

The turret traverse handwheel was located in front and above the gunner's seat.[506] It was normally operated by the gunner's left hand, but this position meant that his wrist chafed against the turret ring casing when traversing the turret. If the gunner let go of the elevation handwheel and used his right hand to turn the turret, he was at risk of cutting it on the sharp edge of the clinometer.[507] Aside from discomfort for the gunner's hands, the wheel did not take a lot of effort to operate due to the high gear ratio. It took two full turns of the handwheel to traverse a single degree. The report describes manually traversing across large angles as "slow and tedious".[508]

The gunner could also traverse the turret by means of the power traverse, controlled by a rocking floor plate. Due to its aforementioned poor placement, the operation of this control was described as "awkward and fatiguing". Quick and accurate control of the turret was described as "almost impossible" in these conditions. To make matters worse, the plate often did not return to neutral when the gunner removed his foot from it. It was also easy to inadvertently tilt the plate and turn the turret when using the elevation handwheel or firing the machine gun using another pedal by the gunner's right foot.[509]

---

[503] WO 291/1003, *Motion Studies of German Tanks*, Section 2, p.2
[504] WO 291/1003, *Motion Studies of German Tanks*, Section 2, p.2
[505] WO 291/1003, *Motion Studies of German Tanks*, Section 2, p.3
[506] WO 291/1003, *Motion Studies of German Tanks*, Section 2, p.2
[507] WO 291/1003, *Motion Studies of German Tanks*, Section 2, p.3
[508] WO 291/1003, *Motion Studies of German Tanks*, Section 2, p.2
[509] WO 291/1003, *Motion Studies of German Tanks*, Section 2, p.3

The gunner's vision devices were inadequate. The rubber brow pad of the T.Z.F.9b gun sight was well shaped, but too hard for comfort and interfered with the gunner's headset when he was aiming. Aside from the gun sight, the gunner had a vision slit facing half-left. According to the report, a block facing forward would have been much more useful.[510]

The gunner's position received a very negative evaluation.

> "In general, the gunner's position is very bad. It is very cramped, the gun controls are badly designed and positioned, and the vision facilities are inadequate."[511]

Like the gunner, the loader's seat had a backrest. His seat was also not adjustable, but it could be folded away under the gun when he needed more room to work. His station was roomy and free of obstructions. This would ostensibly make reloading the main gun easier, but reloading the coaxial MG-34 was very difficult owing to the fact that it was mounted so closely to the main gun.[512]

The loader had a festoon lamp fitted above his seat. The lighting it offered was poor. When operating in semi-darkness or overcast weather, the loader was unable to see the ammunition in the pannier racks.[513]

The loader's sole vision device was a vision slit, much like the gunner's. It too pointed off-center, but this time this was considered an advantage, as it covered a portion of the commander's blind spot. Other than the difficulty in loading the machine gun, the loader's position was found to be satisfactory.[514]

---

[510] WO 291/1003, *Motion Studies of German Tanks*, Section 2, p.3
[511] WO 291/1003, *Motion Studies of German Tanks*, Section 2, p.3
[512] WO 291/1003, *Motion Studies of German Tanks*, Section 2, p.4
[513] WO 291/1003, *Motion Studies of German Tanks*, Section 2, p.5
[514] WO 291/1003, *Motion Studies of German Tanks*, Section 2, p.4

Study of the loader's position also included a loading trial. Two experienced British loaders were given instructions for their particular tank and some time to practice the loading drill.[515]

The report noted that no ammunition was carried in the turret, and the loader had to bend down and retrieve ammunition from a bin to load the gun. Depending on the position of the turret, the loader had between 20 and 46 rounds of ammunition available to him. The largest bins in the panniers held 16 rounds in rows of 4.[516] The top 4 rounds were easily accessible, but each subsequent row was much more difficult to retrieve both due to the depth of the bin and the supporting arms getting in the way. The strips running in between the supporting arms presented a danger in and of themselves, with both loaders injuring themselves on them during the trial. Retrieving rounds further in the bin was also more difficult than closer ones.[517] A round from the top row could be picked up in as little as 1.5-2 seconds, while it took up to 16-18 seconds to pick up a round from the bottom row. It also took an additional 1-3.5 seconds to unlock the clips holding the rounds. The total time to open the clips, procure a round, and load it into the gun could be carried out in as little as 6 seconds or as much as 24.3 seconds, depending on the round that had to be retrieved.[518] On average, it took 6.3-12.4 seconds to load the first 4 rounds in a volley of 16, but 11-16.7 seconds to load the last 4.[519] Note that this procedure did not include several steps that would have to take place in a live fire scenario, such as correcting aim or discarding spent brass.[520] Nevertheless, one can see that the Tiger's rate of fire would decrease significantly as it fought, without the ability to replenish the burst rate of fire by refilling an easily accessible ammunition rack in the turret.

Unlike the turret crew, the driver of the Tiger tank had a seat that could be adjusted back and forth. The angle of the backrest was also adjustable, and it could be dropped to allow for easier access into the turret. The seat could not be elevated into a travel position. Like the gunner and commander, the driver

---

[515] WO 291/1003, *Motion Studies of German Tanks*, Section 1
[516] WO 291/1003, *Motion Studies of German Tanks*, Section 2, p.9
[517] WO 291/1003, *Motion Studies of German Tanks*, Section 2, p.10
[518] WO 291/1003, *Motion Studies of German Tanks*, Section 2, p.11
[519] WO 291/1003, *Motion Studies of German Tanks*, Section 2, p.23
[520] WO 291/1003, *Motion Studies of German Tanks*, Section 2, p.11

had inadequate leg room, with his legs cramped by the steering band casings. The driver's main vision device consisted of a vision block in the front of the hull. It could be covered partially or fully by a steel shutter adjusted by a handwheel. The vision from this device was only satisfactory when the shutter was fully opened. A backup periscope was installed in the driver's hatch, but it faced half-left rather than forward.[521]

The bow gunner had a similar seat to the driver, but it had a smaller and less comfortable backrest. His knees were also cramped by the steering band casings. The bow gunner's position was further made uncomfortable by the poorly balanced machine gun mounting. Despite a compensating spring, it was still breech heavy, with the headpan pressing heavily on the gunner's head causing acute discomfort. Other than that, the bow gunner's position was spacious and comfortable. The radio set installed to the gunner's left atop the gearbox was easily accessible. Unlike the main gun sight, the brow pad of the K.Z.F.2 sight of the bow machine gun was soft and satisfactory. In addition to the machine gun sight, the bow gunner had a fixed periscope to look through, pointing half-right. The British found this unsatisfactory, since if the periscope was pointing forward then the bow gunner could spot targets without using the uncomfortable headpan.[522]

The report concluded with a negative evaluation of all crew positions, particularly the gunner. All workspaces in the tank were restricted and uncomfortable, with the exception of the loader, but even his work was made more difficult by a poor design of the ammunition bins.[523]

The Tiger was not alone in this evaluation. All three vehicles examined (the Panther, Tiger, and Tiger II) suffered from largely the same weaknesses when it came to the comfort of the crew.

---

[521] WO 291/1003, *Motion Studies of German Tanks*, Section 2, p.4
[522] WO 291/1003, *Motion Studies of German Tanks*, Section 2, p.5
[523] WO 291/1003, *Motion Studies of German Tanks*, Section 2, p.13

"(a) Little consideration has been given, in the design of these vehicles, for the comfort of the gunner, and most of the crew's controls are so positioned as to be operated only with discomfort and fatigue. A short study of each vehicle's mock-up by a physiologist would have revealed most of these undesirable qualities.

(b) The gunner and bow-gunner should have adequate vision facilities; in all three tanks this is not possible with the equipment provided.

(c) The ammunition bin fittings are badly designed in all three tanks; hence, loading times are high, and the loaders are more prone to injury than they would be when loading from well-planned bins."[524]

---

[524] WO 291/1003, *Motion Studies of German Tanks*, Abstract

Metallurgical Analysis

Just like the Soviets, the British and Americans tested the Tiger's armor in more ways than just shooting at it. In May of 1943 four samples were taken from a Tiger tank captured in Tunisia: two of nominally 82 mm thick armor and two of nominally 62 mm thick armor. The chemical composition of the 82 mm thick plates was as follows.[525] German standards for this thickness of armor plate are attached for convenience.

	C	Mn	Si	Cr	Ni	Mo	V	P	S
German req. for 55-80 mm armor prior to Nov. 1944	0.37 - 0.47	0.55 - 0.85	Up to 0.4	1.25 - 1.55	-	0.4 - 0.6	0.15 - 0.3	Up to 0.05	Up to 0.05
Super-structure side, 82 mm	0.55	0.73	0.33	2.23	0.05	0.37	-	0.023	0.018
Turret side, 82 mm	0.47	0.70	0.32	2.64	0.04	0.59	-	0.033	0.015
Glacis plate, 62 mm	0.52	0.65	0.28	2.35	0.05	0.59	-	0.018	0.017
Hull side, 62 mm	0.49	0.67	0.30	2.62	0.05	0.52	-	0.027	0.012

Unlike in the Soviet Tigers, which had less carbon than the standard at the time required, the British Tigers had more than required in each plate. Both British and Soviet Tigers showed an excess of chromium and traces of nickel. On the other hand, no vanadium was present in Soviet or British samples.

---

[525] Canadian Military Headquarters, London (CMHQ), Files Block No. 55 - 5775, Image 3421

The British shared this information with the Soviets. In the memo, it is mentioned that the armor is no longer surface hardened and is much softer than what was seen on German tanks previously.[526] 26 mm thick horizontal plates were hardened to 298-343 BHN, which ranges from below the required hardness to nearly the upper end of the scale (311-352 BHN for 16-30 mm steel).[527] Thicker vertical plates ranged from 257 to 310 BHN. This also falls within the acceptable ranges (266-311 BHN for 50-80 mm thick plates and 229-265 BHN for 85-120 mm thick plates), although it could fall out of specification depending on the thickness of the plates.[528]

Likewise, a number of samples were recovered and examined by the Americans. Samples from three different Tiger tanks were provided by the Aberdeen Proving Grounds.[529] Thicknesses are converted from inches and rounded to the nearest millimeter. For the reader's convenience, the data is arranged into three tables with the requirements for German steel for that range of thicknesses.

---

[526] TsAMO RF F.38 Op.11355 D.2704 L.3
[527] A. Volgin, *Tolstaya shkura nemetskogo zverya*, https://warspot.ru/16322-tolstaya-shkura-nemetskogo-zverintsa, retrieved on November 4th, 2023
[528] A. Volgin, *Tolstaya shkura nemetskogo zverya*, https://warspot.ru/16322-tolstaya-shkura-nemetskogo-zverintsa, retrieved on November 4th, 2023
[529] L.H. Grenell and others, Examination of Enemy Materiel (OD-113)(AC-77)(N-119) *Metallurgical Examination of German Tank Armor Plate*, Battelle Memorial Institute, 1945

	BHN	C	Mn	Si	Cr	Ni	Mo	V	P	S
German req. for 35-50 mm armor Nov. 1944	279-324	0.43 - 0.53	0.55 - 0.85	Up to 0.4	1.25 - 1.55	-	0.4 - 0.6	0.15 - 0.3	up to 0.05	up to 0.05
After Nov. 1944		0.41 - 0.49	0.6 - 1	0.5 - 0.8	0.75 - 1.05	-	-	-	up to 0.05	up to 0.05
Tiger #1 upper hull front, 38 mm	339-352	0.46	0.65	0.27	2.42	0.05	0.53	-	0.03	0.014

BHN = Brinell Hardness Number

Only one 38 mm thick plate was taken from the three tanks, although it is not clear where it came from as no part of the Tiger's front is normally 38 mm thick. Nevertheless, the plate is mostly consistent with German pre-November 1944 standards. As seen in the British-examined plates, the chromium content is much higher than expected and vanadium is missing entirely despite being required. The plate is also much harder than expected for this thickness.

	BHN	C	Mn	Si	Cr	Ni	Mo	V	P	S
German requirements for 55-80 mm armor before November 1944	266-311	0.37 - 0.47	0.55 - 0.85	Up to 0.4	1.25 - 1.55	-	0.4 - 0.6	0.15 - 0.3	up to 0.05	up to 0.05
After November 1944		0.41 - 0.49	0.8 - 1.2	0.2 - 0.5	0.9 - 1.2				up to 0.05	up to 0.05
Tiger #1 upper hull right, 83 mm	337-339	0.46	0.76	0.29	2.6	0.06	0.6	-	0.029	0.015
Tiger #1 upper hull left, 83 mm	313-325	0.45	0.61	0.24	2.21	0.06	0.56	-	0.03	0.012
Tiger #1 hull rear, 83 mm	325-343	0.48	0.55	0.23	1.93	0.06	0.55	-	0.017	0.015
Tiger #2 lower hull right, 67 mm	295-326	0.38	0.3	0.23	2.14	0.38	0.18	-	0.015	0.01
Tiger #2 lower hull left, 64 mm	309-311	0.41	0.33	0.33	2.15	0.5	0.21	-	0.014	0.012
Tiger #3 lower hull right, 64 mm	297	0.44	0.72	0.32	1.92	0.06	-	0.047	0.017	0.012
Tiger #3 lower hull left, 64 mm	275-297	0.37	0.68	0.29	1.72	0.06	-	0.061	0.017	0.013

BHN = Brinell Hardness Number

Like the thinner plate, the side and rear armor have too much chromium, although the excess is not quite as egregious. While the thicker plates are harder than expected, the thinner ones are within specifications, albeit on the high side. Both the left and right lower sides of Tiger #2 lack sufficient molybdenum and manganese content and lack vanadium completely. The lower sides of Tiger #3 have no molybdenum and only trace amounts of vanadium. These seemingly small changes in the chemical composition of the metal resulted in different crystalline structures, reducing the steel's ductility and toughness.[530]

---

[530] International Molybdenum Association, *Molybdenum and its Applications - Iron, Steel, and Other Alloys*, https://www.imoa.info/molybdenum-uses/molybdenum-grade-stainless-steels/molybdenum-stainless-steels.php, retrieved on February 16th, 2024

	BHN	C	Mn	Si	Cr	Ni	Mo	V	P	S
German requirements for 85-120 mm before June 1944		0.32 - 0.42	0.3 - 0.65	0.15 - 0.5	2 - 2.4	-	0.2 - 0.3	-	up to 0.05	up to 0.05
After June 1944	220-265	0.37-0.47	0.6 - 0.9	0.2 - 0.5	1.6 - 1.9	-	-	up to 0.15	up to 0.05	up to 0.05
Tiger #1 upper hull front, 102 mm	292-297	0.43	0.57	0.31	2.42	0.05	0.56	-	0.019	0.017
Tiger #1 lower hull front, 102 mm	292-295	0.45	0.6	0.28	2.21	0.05	0.54	-	0.021	0.013
Tiger #2 upper hull front, 102 mm	288-302	0.46	0.47	0.3	2.25	0.51	0.17	0.029	0.01	0.008
Tiger #2 lower hull front, 114 mm	271-278	0.4	0.29	0.25	2.26	0.38	0.2	-	0.07	0.016
Tiger #3 upper hull front, 102 mm	300-304	0.36	0.33	0.26	2.2	0.06	0.21	0.070	0.022	0.013
Tiger #3 lower hull front, 102 mm	252-277	0.43	0.47	0.27	1.91	0.05	0.21	0.023	0.025	0.013
Tiger #3 gun shield, 114 mm	255	0.37	0.55	0.26	2.43	0.14	0.21	0.12	0.038	0.014

BHN = Brinell Hardness Number

Chromium content is still high for the thick front armor, but that is to be expected. One plate even has less chromium than required. Carbon content is high, sometimes in excess of requirements. The Tiger #2 front hull plate, strangely thicker than expected, has slightly less manganese than required. Tiger #2's front hull plates also have a considerable quantity of nickel in them, while others have only trace amounts. The same can be seen in other, thinner plates used in Tiger #2. Molybdenum content varies wildly, some plates have this element in excess, others fall below the requirement. The amount of molybdenum is consistent within each Tiger tank. Most of the samples taken from the front armor are harder than required, and the few within specification are on the high end of the spectrum.

While the Americans did not get different performance with plates from the same tank like the British did in penetration tests and Soviets did in metallurgical tests, their data shows that the composition of armor used in German heavy tanks was very inconsistent. This phenomenon was not unique to the Tiger tank, as out of three Panther tanks tested at Isigny the upper front plates of two tanks shattered after a few hits while the third withstood 30 hits without cracking.[531]

---

[531] N. Moran, *US Army Anti-Armor Firing Tests of 1944*, https://worldoftanks.com/en/news/history/chieftains-hatch-us-guns-vs-german-armor-part-1/, retrieved on December 15th, 2023

Conclusions

American and British troops had the luxury of being able to study the Tiger in two campaigns where they were only encountered in small numbers: Tunisia and Italy. This resulted in an environment where sufficient samples could be retrieved for study with no rush to discover the tank's weaknesses. Fortunately, it turned out that the tank was vulnerable to existing anti-tank guns: the British 17-pounder and American 3" gun. On the flip side, as a result of the Tiger's rarity, weapons fielded to defeat it were not as common as one would have hoped. Despite already having tanks with a 57 mm 6-pounder gun that proved to be effective against the Tiger's armor, the British opted instead to produce tanks with a multipurpose 75 mm gun that had reduced armor piercing performance in exchange for a significantly more useful HE shell. Instead, a large number of tanks and tank destroyers armed with 17-pounders, chiefly converted from American vehicles, were available to tackle heavy armor wherever it was encountered.

The Americans went a similar way. Despite development of first a high velocity 76 mm and then a 90 mm tank gun, Sherman tanks on the front lines continued to use the same 75 mm gun that was only capable of penetrating the Tiger's side armor at close range. The armor piercing performance of this weapon was sufficient for any other mission, and it was thought that in the rare case that Tiger tanks are encountered, they could be dealt with by tank destroyers. In a way, the Americans were correct. While Medium Tanks M4A1(76)W were rushed to the front lines in July of 1944, it was because of the prevalence of the Panther tank rather than the much rarer Tiger.

In a way, the Americans were right. Encounters with Tiger tanks in Normandy were vanishingly rare and sightings of the tank were mostly falsely identified Pz.Kpfw.IV tanks with spaced armor that gave them a very similar silhouette.[532] Steven Zaloga identified just three instances in the fighting between Normandy

---

[532] WW2 Armor, *Every Tank a Tiger*,
https://static1.squarespace.com/static/5d1810846e4b69000116772f/t/628bff3ddfe69644a55eb5dc/1653342015793/Every+Tank+a+Tiger.pdf, retrieved on December 14th, 2023

and VE-Day where American troops encountered a Tiger tank.[533] Nevertheless, the Tiger cemented itself in public consciousness. The image of a Tiger tank as a nigh-invincible enemy force is common in iconic WW2 movies such as Kelly's Heroes, Saving Private Ryan, and, more recently, Fury.

"Tiger" tank built on a T-34 chassis, IWM Duxford. The popularity of the Tiger tank and scarcity of authentic vehicles makes movie makers resort to mockups that use a more readily available chassis. *(Peter Samsonov)*

---

[533] T. Schwallie, *Interview with Steven Zaloga*, https://tankandafvnews.com/2015/01/27/zaloga_interview/, retrieved on February 16th, 2024

Myth or Legend?

The Tiger appeared in North Africa and on the Soviet-German Front almost simultaneously. The Anglo-American armies and the Soviets also had weapons of similar effectiveness that could fight it: high velocity 57 mm anti-tank guns that could penetrate the Tiger's front armor from close up or its sides from medium range as well as 75-76 mm guns mounted on medium tanks that could only penetrate the side armor at close range. Both also had towed guns (85 mm 52-K and 76 mm 17-pounder respectively) that could penetrate even the Tiger's front armor at long range, but were not mounted in an armored vehicle.

The Allies reacted quickly to this new threat. By the end of 1943, the Red Army began to receive tank destroyers and heavy tanks with the new 85 mm D-5 gun and the British began projects to convert American M4 tanks and M10 tank destroyers to carry their 17-pounder. Interestingly enough, while the Red Army quickly adopted a medium tank armed with an 85 mm gun capable of fighting Tiger tanks, the British and Americans were in no rush. Both had specialized vehicles capable of defeating heavy armor and did not consider the Tiger to be a widespread phenomenon due to encountering only small numbers of these tanks in North Africa and in Sicily. The British transitioned their infantry and cruiser tanks to multipurpose 75 mm guns with lower armor penetration than their 6-pounder guns, and while the Americans developed and produced Sherman tanks with high velocity 76 mm guns, there was no urgency to put them into battle until almost two months into the invasion of Normandy. The difference in attitude towards 57 mm guns is an interesting contrast in the anti-Tiger strategies of the two nations, although the British did continue to develop improved ammunition for their 6-pounder which enabled it to destroy Tiger tanks at greater range.

While the Tiger's thick armor and long range gun were powerful weapons on the battlefield, they compared favorably only to medium tanks half their weight. The Soviets, British, and Americans all developed heavy tanks of their own with superior armor (and, aside from the British, armament) at a much lower weight. The Tiger also ceased to be the Allies' greatest concern, as the Germans themselves developed a tank with thicker front armor and a more powerful gun: the Panther. Most importantly, the Panther was available in much greater numbers, making it a greater concern for Soviet, American, and British tankers and anti-tank gunners.

The Tiger's potential on the battlefield was also sapped by design and manufacturing flaws. The engine and transmission never became sufficiently reliable throughout its service life, often leading to breakdowns at the most inconvenient time. The heavy tank was very difficult to tow even for another Tiger, and a lack of armored recovery halftracks meant that Tiger tanks disabled by relatively minor battle damage or mechanical faults had to be demolished or abandoned. Declining quality of German steel also meant that the Tiger's thick armor plates did not offer the formidable protection that might have been expected from them on paper. A poor arrangement of vision devices heavily impaired the Tiger's observation, and the confined workspace and badly laid out controls impeded the effectiveness of its crew.

Despite the layman's impression of a Tiger as a solitary hunter on the battlefield, it could never operate in this fashion. The Tiger's heavy weight, poor off-road performance, low reliability, and poor vision required these tanks to operate only with a screen of medium tanks, support from artillery, engineering reconnaissance, and infantry for close defense.

However, all of these weaknesses offered little consolation to the crew of a Sherman or a T-34 tank that came face to face with a Tiger in an advantageous position. Even though Tigers were a rare sight on the battlefield, the majority of Allied tankers never received a weapon that allowed them to fight this tank as an equal. It was the fear of this incredibly unlikely but potentially fatal encounter that elevated the Tiger to the near-mythological status it holds today, rather than the inability of Allied armies to deal with this heavy tank on the battlefield.

Appendix 1: Glossary

ABTU: *Avto-bronetankovoye Upravleniye*, Automobile, Armored Vehicle, and Tank Directorate. Formed on November 22nd, 1934 to manage design, testing, and production of armored and unarmored vehicles for the army, as well as training in their use. Reformed into the GABTU (Glavnoye Avto-bronetankovoye Upravleniye, Main Automobile, Armored Vehicle, and Tank Directorate) on June 26th, 1940. After reorganization in December of 1942 the GBTU (Glavnoye Bronetankovoye Upravleniye, Main Armored Vehicle and Tank Directorate) was responsible only for managing tank design, testing, and production.

AP: Armor Piercing. A shot or shell primarily designed for penetration of armor. AP shells contain a small bursting charge to shatter the shell into fragments after penetration that destroy the crew and the tank's internal components. This type of shell is also called AP-HE. In contrast, AP shot contains no explosive charge and relies on fragments of armor generated during penetration to deal damage inside the tank.

APC: Armor Piercing Capped. A shot or shell primarily designed for penetration of armor equipped with a soft cap to prevent the core of the projectile from shattering against hard armor on impact.

APCBC: Armor Piercing Capped Ballistic Cap. An armor piercing shot or shell with a ballistic cap to give it improved aerodynamic qualities in flight and a soft cap to prevent the core of the projectile from shattering against hard armor on impact.

APCR: Armor Piercing Composite Rigid. An armor piercing shot consisting of a penetrating core made of a hard alloy like tungsten carbide surrounded by a lightweight sabot. The sabot is rigidly attached to the core and only comes off on impact. Lighter weight of the shot compared to a standard AP shell results in higher muzzle velocity and better penetration at short ranges, but as lighter projectiles lose speed more rapidly, APCR is ineffective at long ranges.

APDS: Armor Piercing Discarding Sabot. An armor piercing shot consisting of a penetrating core made of a hard alloy like tungsten carbide surrounded by a lightweight sabot. The sabot comes off as soon as the shot exits the barrel.

Ballistic Limit: In British practice, the velocity at which half of all shells or shot hitting an armor plate create a hole or crack through which daylight can be seen, and half of which only create a dent or incomplete crack.

GABTU: See ABTU.

GAU: *Glavonoye Artilleriyeskoye Upravleniye*, Main Artillery Directorate. This organization was in charge of developing all sorts of artillery, including tank guns and SPGs.

GBTU: See ABTU.

GKO alternatively **GOKO:** *Gosudarstvenniy Komitet Oborony*, State Committee of Defense. This was the highest ranking entity in charge of defense production and organization in 1941-1945.

GMC: Gun Motor Carriage, the American designation for self propelled artillery.

HEAT: High Explosive, Anti Tank. A type of shell that penetrates armor by focusing the energy produced by a high explosive blast on one point. Since penetration is achieved through chemical energy, the impact velocity is not important and HEAT shells can effectively be used by low velocity weapons like howitzers. However, the steep ballistic curve resulting from low velocity makes it harder to heat a target like a tank.

HVAP: High Velocity Armor Piercing. See APCR.

Mission kill: Damage to a vehicle that does not destroy it, but makes it unable to fight effectively, such as by destroying the running gear or the gun.

Mobility kill: Damage to a vehicle that does not destroy it, but renders it immobile. See Mission kill.

OKH: *Oberkommando des Heeres*, Supreme Command of the Army.

Platoon: the smallest tactical unit of tanks on the battlefield. Typically composed of 5 tanks, although platoons in Tiger battalions were made up of four vehicles.

schwere Panzer-Abteilung also abbreviated as s.Pz.Abt: heavy tank battalion. Tiger tanks were chiefly employed in this formation.

Shell: A hollow projectile filled with explosives.

Shot: A solid projectile typically intended for the penetration of armor without an explosive filler.

SPG: Self Propelled Gun.

Subcaliber AP: See APCR.

W/R Limit: In British practice, the velocity below which the shell or shot hitting an armor plate is expected to form a penetration, but not pass clean through the plate (code R), and above which the shell or shot passes clean through the plate (code W).

Appendix 2: Preliminary Instructions on Combating Tigers

USSR People's Commissariat of Defense

Artillery Command Directorate of the 16th Army

Operations Department

July 15th, 1943

#01321

I supply you with some preliminary conclusions on the destruction of T-VI "Tiger" tanks.

During the fighting on the Orel-Kursk axis and on our sector of the front, it was discovered that German T-VI tanks are quite vulnerable to 76 mm and 45 mm guns.

1. The tank is incapacitated when hit in the side or turret with armor piercing shells from the 76 mm gun at ranges of up to 800 m.
2. The tank is incapacitated when hit in the side at ranges up to 1 km with subcaliber shot from the 76 mm gun.
3. The front of the tank is not always penetrated with subcaliber shot at ranges of over 800 m.
4. The best results with a 45 mm gun firing subcaliber shot are obtained when hitting the side, running gear, and engine compartment at ranges of up to 200 m.
5. The maximum effective range is 500-600m.

Tactics developed to engage Tiger tanks should consider the following nuances.

1. Tiger tanks always escort light and medium tanks.
2. If T-VI tanks are deployed in small groups, they will follow the flanks of their formation. If they are deployed in large numbers, then they will be at the head.

3. When fighting along roads, the T-VI will keep to the column's wake and cover the other tanks from anti-tank guns positioned along the roads. There were cases when tanks fighting along the road were covered with smokescreens.
4. The T-VI are covered by SPGs with fire and maneuver. They are typically positioned on heights and fire from a range of 1-1.5 kilometers.
5. To cover the T-VI from the air, the enemy includes AA guns in tank formations, a part of which follows the tanks.
6. It is known that when faced with powerful anti-tank defenses, the T-VI will attempt to bypass it.

Knowing all this, one must:

1. Strike at the flanks of small tank groups first. This is where the T-VI will be, as a rule. In large groups, destroy the tanks at the head first. As instructed before, finish off knocked out tanks. Reliably shoot them up, render them completely useless, do not give the enemy a chance to restore them.
2. Allocate special guns or batteries to combat the SPGs supporting the T-VI.
3. Thoroughly study and report on methods of combating the T-VI.

Chief of Staff, Guards Colonel Belyaev

Chief of the Operations Department, Guards Major Nikolskiy

- TsAMO RF F.9623 Op.1 D.27 L.60-61

Appendix 3: Memo to Soldiers, Sergeants, and Officers on Combat with German "Ferdinand" SPGs and "Tiger" Tanks[534]

In attempts to hold back our advance and delay the hour of his death, the enemy will undertake counterattacks with tanks and SPGs.

Soldier! Sergeant! Officer! Remember that the success in battle depends on your courage and ability to combat tanks and SPGs!

Russians have always said: "The devil is not as black as he is painted!"[535] - The Tiger and Ferdinand are great machines, but their feet are weak!

Rifleman! Don't be distracted, disguise yourself, let the Tiger approach, and throw an anti-tank grenade at his tracks or drive sprocket! If one is not enough, do not spare a second!

Your brother in arms Guardsman Anatoliy Uglovskiy stopped a Tiger with a grenade, he is a hero!

Red Armyman Smischuk is a hero! He let the tank approach his trench, blew up the track with a grenade, and threw a bottle[536] at its rear. The tank may be

---

[534] TsAMO RF F.358 Op.5916 D.716 L.124-125

[535] The Russian variant of the idiom literally translates as "the devil is not as frightening as he is in paintings". Here and afterwards the colloquial style of the original is preserved as much as possible.

[536] Molotov cocktails were officially referred to as "bottles of incendiary fluid" in Soviet manuals.

big, but it still bursts into flames. A good lather is half a shave![537] A second tank comes after the first, and there is the third. All will burn the same. A brave and skilled man fears no tank. A unit with such a soldier is honored and the soldier receives glory.

Are you any worse than them? Fight more fiercely, don't spare yourself. Victory won't come to you, you have to take it yourself!

Tigers and Ferdinands don't see well. Strike their observation ports with fire from your rifle, machine gun, or anti-tank rifle, strike at the machine's eyes! You will blind the tank and wound the crew! Fire your anti-tank rifle at the commander's cupola and the cannon! You will jam the cupola or damage the cannon.

If you see that the tank has disguised itself, show the target to the artillery with tracers or flares.

Sapper-miner! Know how to quickly set up mines ahead of Tigers and Ferdinands! The mine will blow up the track or floor of the vehicle. Prepare surprises for the Tigers and Ferdinands! Tie a mine to a cord and wait in a trench. If the tank is not coming straight at you, pull the mine underneath it. Patience and skill are the main things in battle!

Artilleryman! You are responsible for your infantry, for your men. Don't spare yourself, strike the Tigers and Ferdinands! Any gun, a battalion[538], regimental[539],

---

[537] The Russian variant of the idiom literally translates as "the beginning is a great trouble".

[538] 45 mm anti-tank guns were originally developed as battalion-level artillery.

[539] 76 mm model 1927 and 1943 regimental guns were small low velocity weapons for close support of infantry.

or divisional gun[540], can strike at the tracks, drive sprockets, and wheels with an armor piercing shell. The tank will stop for sure!

Battalion gunner! Small rain lays great dust![541] Try to strike at the Tiger from the side. Load the subcaliber round, hide yourself, and wait! Let the tank approach to 200 meters, roll out your gun quickly. Your steady hand and eye will decide the rest. Our shells are welded from tough steel, they will penetrate the side of the Tiger and find the Germans behind it.

Strike the Ferdinand like Guardsman Sagombayev!

Riflemen, don't hesitate, don't let the Germans leave the burning vehicle. Get them in your sights and take them down!

Regimental 76 mm gunner! Be quick in your movements and sharp of eye! Let the tank or SPG approach to 500-700 meters, don't rush, fire seldom, but precisely.

If the tank is coming towards you, it's best to shoot at the running gear. If it's driving past you, fire a HEAT shell at the side armor!

The German machine is strong, no doubt, skill and Russian savvy are needed to stop it.

---

[540] 76 mm F-22, USV, and ZIS-3 guns were higher velocity weapons that were also useful in an anti-tank role. Divisional artillery also included 122 mm M-30 howitzers, which fired a potent HEAT shell.

[541] The Russian variant of this idiom literally translates as "small, but mighty"

Fire at the base of the turret or at the armament with any gun, you will force the German to stop firing.

Divisional 76 mm gunner! Your weapon is a menace for tanks and Ferdinands![542] No matter which way the Tiger turns, you can penetrate its armor! If you want to strike its front, don't rush, let it come within 100-200 meters and then knock the wind out of it with one shot!

It's better to shoot the Ferdinand in the side. Aim for its vulnerable points, the side armor and running gear. In case of the Tiger, shoot its turret as well. If the Ferdinand is coming towards you, time your shot and fire at the running gear, at the lower sloped armor, and at the gun.

Artilleryman! Do not fall behind your infantry, cover it from tanks and Ferdinands! To knock out German vehicles successfully, hide yourself well and pick positions carefully to not expose yourself to fire needlessly!

Artillery officer! A lot depends on you in battle. The troops look up to you in difficult times. Be calm, brave, and skillful. Grab German Tigers and Ferdinands in pincers of fire! Do not let a single one escape!

Keep in touch with infantry, bail them out, but don't get complacent. Support the infantry, earn its gratitude, that's the main thing! Cooperation is power!

Soldier! Sergeant! Officer! Bravely meet the counterattacking enemy and strike him skillfully, do not hesitate!

---

[542] The term "Ferdinand" is used interchangeably to refer both to the *Panzerjäger Tiger (P)* tank destroyer specifically and German tank destroyers in general.

The people look at you with pride and hope. The people need victory and peace!

- Political department of the Army.

June 18th, 1944. "Sons of the Motherland" newspaper printers.

Bibliography

Primary Sources

Russian Language Sources

RGASPI F.644 Op.2 D.105 L.24, Dokument 2457ss. *O sryve postavok zagotovok i litya artilliriyskikh sistem Uralmashzavodom Narkomata tankovoy promyshlennosti zavodu #8 Narkomata vooryzheniya*

RGASPI F.644 Op.2 D.138 L.194-197, Dokument 2943ss. *Ob izgotovlenii opytnykh obraztsov tankov IS*

RGASPI F.644 Op.2 D.156 L.92-95, Dokument 3290ss. *O vosstanovlenii proizvodstva 122-mm korpusnyh pushek obrazca 1931-1937 g. i izgotovlenii opytnyh obrazcov legkih korpusnyh pushek.*

RGASPI F.644 Op.2 D.165 L.88-91, Dokument 3289ss. *Ob usilenii artilleeriyskogo vooruzheniya tankov i samokhodnykh ustanovok*

RGASPI F.644 Op.2 D.170 L.177, Dokument 3373ss. Rasporyazheniye. *Ob izgotovlenii seriynoy partii 122-mm kumulyativnykh i 152-mm broneboynyno-trassiruyuschikh snaryadov*

RGASPI F.644 Op.2 D.202 L.135-138 Dokument 3891ss, *O proizvodstve tankov KV c 85-mm pushkoy (KV-85)*

RGASPI F.644 Op.2 D.202 L.139, Dokument 3982ss. Ob organizatsii proizvodstva 85-mm samokhodnykh artustanovok na baze tanka T-34 na Uralmashzavode

RGASPI F.644 Op.2 D.239 L.101, Dokument 4479ss O tyazhelom tanke IS-2 so 122-mm pushkoy

RGASPI F.644 Op.2 D.252 L.140-147, Dokument 4776ss. O proizvodstve tankov T-34-85 s 85-mm pushkoy na zavode #112 Narkomata tankovoy promyshlennosti

RGASPI F.644 Op.2 D.255 L.104-108, Dokument 4873ss. O vooruzhenii tankov T-34 85-mm pushkoy vzamen 76-mm F-34

RGASPI F.644 Op.2 D.349 L.43, Dokument 6131ss. Ob organizatsii proizvodstva samokhodnykh artilleriyskikh ustanovok SU-100 na Uralmashzavoda Narkomata tankovoy promyshlennosti i 100-mm pushek D-10s na zavodakh ##8 i 9 Narkomata vooruzheniya

TsAMO RF F.38 Op.11355 D.949 L., *Tanki - Opytniye obraztsy*

TsAMO RF F.38 Op.11353 D.951 L.1, *Taktiko-tekhnicheskiye kharakteristiki opytnykh obraztsov pushek, ustanavlivayemykh na tankakh germanskoy armii*

TsAMO RF F.38 Op.11355 D.1377 L.195, *Report on experimental factory #100 projects for June 1943*

TsAMO RF F.38 Op.11355 D.1545 L.9-10, *Obstrel korpusov tankov KV-1 i T-34 iz 88 mm pushki*

TsAMO RF F.38 Op.11355 D.1712 L.31, *Vypiska iz itogovoy razvedsvodki #2 UBT i MV Volkhovskogo Fronta za period s 15.1 po 31.1.43*

TsAMO RF F.38 Op.11355 D.2704 L.3, *Tendentsii v proizvodstve germanskikh bronevykh plit /vyderzhka iz doklada prigotovlennogo Nachalnikom Glavnogo Britanskogo Upravleniya po Proyektirovaniyu Tankov/*

TsAMO RF F.38 Op.11355 D.2890 L.1, *Rezultaty zamerov usiliy na rychayakh upravleniya inostrannykh i otechestvennykh tankov*

TsAMO RF F.38 Op.11369 D.28 L.1-41, *Zaklucheniye kommissii po ispytaniyu 100 mm tankovykh pushek D-10-T i S-34-T ustanovlennykh v tankakh IS*

TsAMO RF F.38 Op.11369 D.490 L.35-38, *Ob ustanovke v tank IS 100 mm pushki D-10 zavoda #9 NKV vmesto 122 mm pushki togo zhe zavoda*

TsAMO RF F.38 Op.11369 D.709 L.3-4, *Dokladnaya zapiska komanduyushego BT i MV KA zamestitelyu predsedatelya gosudarstvennogo komiteta oborony L.P. Berii po rezultatam ispytaniy broneboynykh snaryadov*

TsAMO RF F.38 Op.11377 D.12 L.1a-61, *Otchet po ispytaniyam bronevoy zaschity nemetskogo tanka T-VI obstrelom*

TsAMO RF F.38 Op.11377 D.129 L.1-50, *Otchet to ispytaniyu snaryadnym obstrelom lobovykh detaley korpusa i bashni nemetskogo tyazhelogo tanka "Tigr B"*

TsAMO RF F.81 Op.12038 D.385 L.69, *Letter from GBTU Chief Lieutenant General Vershinin to GAU Chief Major General of Artillery Yakovlev*

TsAMO RF F.81 Op.12038 D.775 L.8, *Oriyentirovochnoye kolichestvo stanko-chasov potrebnoye dlya vypolneniya rabot /pri melko-seriynom proizvodstve/*

TsAMO RF F.81 Op.12063 D.19 L.155-156, *Letter from Assistant Chief of Department #16 of the GAU Artillery Committee Engineer-Major Solomonov to Chief of Department #16 of the GAU Artillery Committee Colonel Zhevanik dated May 31st, 1943*

TsAMO RF F.81 Op.12063 D.1 L.45, *Letter from Chief of OKB-172 Lieutenant Colonel K.A. Ivanov to the Chairman of the NKV Technical Council Satel, Chairman of the Artillery Council Hohlov, and Commissar of State Security Kravchenko dated October 2nd, 1943*

TsAMO RF F.81 Op.12104 D.201 L.11-12, *Letter from the GAU UVKA Chief Military Engineer 1st Class Lipin to the director of the Kirov Factory in Leningrad dated March 13th, 1941*

TsAMO RF F.81 Op.12104 D.261 L.7-12, *Otchet po razrabotke i sostavleniyu tablits broneprobivayemosti betonoboynymi snaryadami 122, 152 i 203 mm kalibra dlya sistem A-10, ML-20 i B-4*

TsAMO RF F.307 Op.4148 D.189 L.107-109, *Letter from the Commander of armored Forces Marshal Fedorenko to the Commander of the 2nd Ukrainian Front Marshal Konev dated April 1st, 1944*

TsAMO RF F.315 Op.4440 D.311 L.239, *Letter from the Chief of Staff of the 3rd Guards Tank Army Major General Bakhmetyev to the Chief of Staff of the 1st Ukrainan Front dated August 31st, 1944*

TsAMO RF F.315 Op.4440 D.311 L.241, *Letter from the Chief of the Operational Department of the 9th Mechanized Corps Guards Colonel Koshevatskiy to the Chief of the Operational Department of the 3rd Guards Tank Army dated August 30th, 1944*

TsAMO RF F.341 Op.5328 D.149 L.155, *Danniye po borbe s tyazhelimi tankami marki "Tigr-6"*

TsAMO RF F.358 Op.5916 D.716 L.124-125, *Pamyatka boytsu, serzhantu, ofitseru o borbe s nemetskimi samokhodnimi orudiyami "Ferdinand" i tankami "Tigr"*

TsAMO RF F.442 Op.8465 D.64 L.29, *Opyt boyevogo ispolzovaniya protivnikom tankov tipa T-6 (Tigr) v nastupatelnom boyu*

TsAMO RF F.500 Op.12480 D.137 L.587-590, *Ausbildungshinweis Nr.14 (Anregungen für den Einsatz von Panzerkampfwagen VI ("Tiger").)*

TsAMO RF F.959 Op.1 D.355 L.16, *Letter from the Chief of Staff of Artillery Lieutenant General Samsonov to Chiefs of Staff of artillery of Fronts and Armies dated April 17th, 1944*

TsAMO RF F.983 Op.1 D.26 L.20-21, *Letter from GAU Chief Colonel-General of Artillery Yakovlev to commanders of artillery of Fronts and Armies dated December 15th, 1943*

TsAMO RF F.1140 Op.1 D.27 L.65, *Letter from Chief of Staff of the 42nd Rifle Division Lieutenant Colonel Komarov to the Chief of Staff of the 33rd Army Major General Kinosin dated May 14th, 1943*

TsAMO RF F.1410 Op.1 D.220 L.113, *Letter from the Chief of Staff of the 160th Tank Destroyer Artillery Battalion captain Derish to the Chief of Staff of the 169th Rifle Division dated January 18th, 1944*

TsAMO RF F.1739 Op.1 D.70 L.443, *Noviy nemetskiy tank tipa T-6 ("Tigr")*

TsAMO RF F.1233 Op.1 D.152 L.51-59, *Instruktsii po primemeniyu 57 mm i 76 mm podalibernykh broneboyno-trassiruyushikh snaryadov i 122 mm broneboyno-prozhigayushego snaryada*

TsAMO RF F.3161 Op.1 D.11 L.66, *Akt-otchet o provedenii boyevykh strelb 2-m tankovym batalyonom 63 GvTBr iz tankov T-34 i T-34-85 po tanku T-6 (Tigr)*

TsAMO RF F.3335 Op.1 D.9 L.213-216, *Protivnikov vypushen i prinyat na vooruzheniye noviy tyazheliy tank T-VI "Tigr"*

TsAMO RF F.3384 Op1. D.13 L.18, *Opyt vedeniya boyev s tankami tipa T-6 "Tigr"*

TsAMO RF F.3408 Op.1 D.30 L.74-76, *Otchet o provedyennykh opytnykh strelb artillerii 9 tk po tanku T-6*

TsAMO RF F.3475 Op.1 D.58 L.427, *Letter from the HQ of the 7th Guards Cavalry Corps to commanders of its composite units dated July 8th, 1943*

TsAMO RF F.3481 Op.1 D.140 L.262, *Letter from Chief of Staff of Artillery of the Transcaucasian Front, Colonel Rymarev to subordinate artillery commanders dated June 10th, 1943*

TsAMO RF F.6231 Op.26929s D.2 L.26-27, *Borba s tankami T-IV (Tigr)*

TsAMO RF F.9604 Op.1 D.38 L.229, *Letter from the GAU Chief Marshal Yakovlev to commanders of artillery of Fronts and Armies dated September 9th, 1943*

TsAMO RF F.9623 Op.1 D.27 L.60-61, *Letter from the Commander of Artillery of the 18th Army to commanders of its composite units dated July 15th, 1943*

TsAMO RF F.9755 Op.1 D.8 L.347-351, *Letter from the Chief of Staff of the 1st Howitzer Artillery Brigade to the Chief of Staff off the 1475th Howitzer Artillery Regiment dated November 9th, 1944*

TsAMO RF F.10895 Op.1 D.7 L.146, *Rezultaty ispytaniya strelby 45 mm orudiya, protivotankovykh ruzhey, i deystviya protivotankhovykh granat po tankam Tigr*

TsAMO RF F.11243 Op.1 D.18 L.87, *Opyt strelby proneprozhigayushimi snaryadami 305 za leto 1944 goda*

English & German Language Sources

Anlage zu H.Dv. 469/3b Panzer-Beschußtafel 8,8 cm KwK 36 as published on February 15th, 1943

Canadian Military Headquarters, London (1939-1947) - 17473, Image 70-71, Letter from Captain W.R. Pacaud to Lt.Col E.D. James dated September 15th, 1942

Canadian Military Headquarters, London (CMHQ), Files Block No. 55 - 5772, Image 4043-4045, *ACIGS(W) Report on Tour to A.F.H.Q. and A.A.I*

Canadian Military Headquarters, London (CMHQ), Files Block No. 55 - 5772, Image 4920-4921, *Appreciation of Effect of Introduction of German PzKw "X" or "Tiger" Tank*

Canadian Military Headquarters, London (CMHQ), Files Block No. 55 - 5773, Image 912-921, *Department of Tank Design Test Bay - First Report on Project R.4248 Performance Tests of Two Stage Oil Bath Air Cleaners for Use on German Tank PzKw VI (Tiger)*

Canadian Military Headquarters, London (CMHQ), Files Block No. 55 - 5773, Image 1391-1400, *German Heavy Tank Pz.Kw.VI(H)*

Canadian Military Headquarters, London (CMHQ), Files Block No. 55 - 5773, Image 1403-1404, *Notes on Tank Tactics*

Canadian Military Headquarters, London (CMHQ), Files Block No. 55 - 5773, Image 1707-1714, *Addendum to Section II - Fighting Arrangements*

Canadian Military Headquarters, London (CMHQ), Files Block No. 55 - 5773, Image 1762-1792, *Part IV - Power Plant*

Canadian Military Headquarters, London (CMHQ), Files Block No. 55 - 5774, Image 3665-3710, *British Army Staff (AFV) Situation Report as on 18.7.43 No.13*

Canadian Military Headquarters, London (CMHQ), Files Block No. 55 - 5774, Image 4190-4147, *British Army Staff (AFV) Situation Report as on 18.1.44 No.18*

Canadian Military Headquarters, London (CMHQ), Files Block No. 55 - 5775, Image 3414-3423, *Technical and Tactical Summary of Foreign A.F.V's and Equipment No.22*

Canadian Military Headquarters, London (CMHQ), Files Block No. 55 - 5775, Image 3631-3654, *Special report on German Pz.Kw.VI "Tiger" Dated 5 June 1943*

Canadian Military Headquarters, London (CMHQ), Files Block No. 55 - 5776, Image 12-19, *Mediterranean Area A.F.V. Technical Report No.21*

Canadian Military Headquarters, London (CMHQ), Files Block No. 55 - 5776, Image 562-593, *Mediterranean Area A.F.V. Technical Report No.24*

Canadian Military Headquarters, London (CMHQ), Files Block No. 55 - 5776, Image 600-632, *Mediterranean Area A.F.V. Technical Report No.23*

Canadian Military Headquarters, London (CMHQ), Files Block No. 55 - 5777, Image 1682-1683, *Appendix 'J' to AFV(T) Report No.7*

Canadian Military Headquarters, London (CMHQ), Files Block No. 55 - 5777, Image 2098-2099, *D.R.A.C. Technical Intelligence Digest No.7*

Canadian Military Headquarters, London (CMHQ), Files Block No. 55 - 5777, Image 2110-2117, *D.R.A.C. Technical Intelligence Digest No.6*

Canadian Military Headquarters, London (CMHQ), Files Block No. 55 - 5777, Image 2193-2202, *D.R.A.C. Technical Intelligence Digest No.1*

Canadian Military Headquarters, London (CMHQ), Files Block No. 55 - 5777, Image 2320-2323, Appendix 'M' to 21 Army Group RAC Liaison Letter No.3

Canadian Military Headquarters, London (CMHQ), Files Block No. 55 - 5777, Image 3909-3935, Committee on the Soft Ground Grossing Performance of Track Laying armored Fighting Vehicles - *Second Interim Report - December 1945*

Canadian Military Headquarters, London (CMHQ), Files Block No. 55 - 5777, Image 3804-3851, National Research Council of Canada - Associate Committee on Soil and Snow Mechanics - *Technical Memorandum No.3 - The Interrelation of Soil Mechanics and the Design and Operation of Vehicles*

Canadian Military Headquarters, London (CMHQ), Files Block No. 55 - 5777, Image 4423-4424, *Heavy Support Tks*

Canadian Military Headquarters, London (CMHQ), Files Block No. 55 - 5778, mage 4262-4267, *Medium Tanks T23, T25, and T26 - Classification as Limited Procurement Types for Procurement of Limited Number of each Recommended.*

Canadian Military Headquarters, London (CMHQ), Files Block No. 55 - 5788, Image 3419, *Penetration vs Homo Plate at 30°*

Canadian Military Headquarters, London (CMHQ), Files Block No. 55 - 5778, Image 4399, *Extract from U.S. Ordnance Committee Minutes Summary No.63A May 27.1943*

Canadian Military Headquarters, London (CMHQ), Files Block No. 55 - 5779, Image 55-57, *Memorandum to President, The Armored Board, Fort Knox, Kentucky dated June 10th, 1944*

CAB 63/166, *Design and production of heavy tanks*

CAB 66/50/12, Select Committee on National Expenditure: *Report on Tank Production*

WO 194/744, *Firing trial in Tunisia against the hull of German Pz Kw VI Tiger tank*

WO 291/1003, *Motion Studies of German Tanks*

DTD Experimental Report AT No.252 armor Branch *Report On Firing Trial against German Tiger Pz.Kw.VI Parts I-IV*

Fighting Vehicle Proving Establishment *Report No. F.T.1553 on Comparative Trials of Various A.F.V's in Soft Ground Conditions*

School of Tank Technology, *Attack on German Panther & Tiger Tanks*

NARA Army Ground Forces HQ Decimal Correspondence 470.8 - Foreign Tanks, *New German Tanks*

NARA Army Ground Forces HQ Decimal Correspondence 470.8 - Tanks, Misc, Excerpt, R.A.C. *Liaison Letter No.3 from the North African Forces*

NARA ETO Technical Intelligence Report No.114, *Vulnerability Charts of German Tanks*

L.H. Grenell and others, Examination of Enemy Materiel (OD-113)(AC-77)(N-119) *Metallurgical Examination of German Tank Armor Plate*, Battelle Memorial Institute, 1945

Secondary Sources

A. Shirokorad, *Artilleriya v Velikoy Otechestvennoy Voyne*, AST, Moscow, 2010

M. Postnikov, *Bronezaschita Tyazhelikh Tankov KV i IS 1941-1945*, Eksprint, Moscow, 2006

N. Moran, *Can Openers*, Echo Point Books & Media, Brattleboro Vermont, 2017. Pp.100-101

H. Boog and others, *Das Deutsche Reich und der Zweite Weltkrieg 6: Der Globale Krieg. Bd. 6*, Deutsche Verlags-Anstalt, Stuttgart, Germany, 1990

B. Kast, Die Organisation der Panzerdivisionen 1939 und 1944 – Quantitative Analyse, in: *Achtung Panzer? Zur Panzerwaffe der Wehrmacht*. Military History Group, 2022

S.J. Zaloga, *M4 (76mm) Sherman Medium Tank 1943-65*, Osprey Publishing, Oxford, 2003. Kindle Edition

Directorate of armored and Mechanized Forces of the Red Army, *Naibolee uyazvimiye i porazhayemiye mesta nemetskogo tanka T-VI i sposoby borby s nim*, Military Publisher of the People's Commissariat of Defense of the USSR, Moscow, 1943

Y. Bakhurin, *Panzerjager Tiger (P) Ferdinand*, Tactical Press, Moscow, 2014

M. Kolomiyets, *T-34 Pervaya polnaya entsiklopediya, Yauza*, Moscow, 2009

United States War Department, *Tactical and Technical Trends, No. 18*, Washington, 1943

United States War Department, *Tactical and Technical Trends, No. 20*, Washington, 1943

Tablitsy strelby 122-mm gaubitsy obr. 1938 g., 5th annotated edition, Military Publisher of the People's Commissariat of Defense, Moscow, 1943

B.O. Newsome, *The Tiger Tank and Allied Intelligence Volume III, Tiger 131: From Africa to Europe*, Tank Archives Press, Coronado, 2020

D. Fletcher, *The Universal Tank*, HMSO, London, 1993

M. Svirin, *Tyazheliy tank Pantera Pz.Kpfw V*, Tseyghaus, Moscow, 2007

M. Svirin, *Tyazheliye tanki IS*, Tseyghaus, Moscow, 2007

A. Ulanov, D. Shein, *Perviye Tridtsatchetverki*, Tactical Press, Moscow, 2014

C.W. Wilbeck, *Sledgehammers Strengths and Flaws of Tiger Tank Battalions in World War II*, The Aberjona Press, Bedford, 2004

H. Doyle and T. Jentz, *Tiger I Heavy Tank 1942-1945*, Oxford: Osprey Publishing, 1993

W. Schneider, *Tigers in Combat I*, Stackpole Books, Mechanicsburg, 2004

Office of the Chief of Ordnance, *Vulnerability Tests of German Tanks Pz Kw III, Pz Kw IV, Pz Kw VI*, 1944

J. Wehner, Waren deutsche Panzer zu teuer?, in: *Achtung Panzer? Zur Panzerwaffe der Wehrmacht*. Military History Group, 2022

Websites

Tank AFVs, *17Pdr SP Achilles*, https://tank-afv.com/ww2/gb/17pdr-SP-Achilles.php, retrieved on February 20th, 2024

Getty Images, 2. World War, Northafrica, theater of war: German tank VI 'Tiger' in Tunis (Tunesia) - December 1942, https://www.gettyimages.co.uk/detail/news-photo/world-war-northafrica-theater-of-war-german-tank-vi-tiger-news-photo/542370013, retrieved on November 6th, 2023

P. Samsonov, *A Firefly with a Stinger*, https://www.tankarchives.ca/2023/03/a-firefly-with-stinger.html, retrieved on December 7th, 2023

P. Samsonov, *Americanskaya zebra protiv nemetskikh tigrov i panter*, https://warspot.ru/18019-amerikanskaya-zebra-protiv-nemetskih-tigrov-i-panter, retrieved on December 11th, 2023

P. Samsonov, *Amerikanskiy Zveroboy*, https://warspot.ru/19927-amerikanskiy-zveroboy, retrieved on December 7th, 2023

Y. Pasholok, *Bolshegoloviy kreyser*, https://warspot.ru/13021-bolshegolovyy-kreyser, retrieved on December 6th, 2023

Y. Pasholok, *Borba za mesto na konveyere*, https://warspot.ru/11457-borba-za-mesto-na-konveyere, retrieved on November 1st, 2023

N.F. Evans, *British Artillery in World War 2, Artillery Organisations*, https://nigelef.tripod.com/RAorg.htm, retrieved on January 11th, 2024

The Tank Museum, *Capture of Tiger 131*, https://tankmuseum.org/article/capture_of_tiger_131, retrieved on November 6th, 2023

P. Samsonov, *Captured German Tanks in the Red Army*, https://www.tankarchives.ca/2016/07/captured-german-tanks-in-red-army.html, retrieved on December 15th, 2023

Y. Pasholok, *Dlinnaya ruka po-angliyski*, https://warspot.ru/5976-dlinnaya-ruka-po-angliyski, retrieved on December 5th, 2023

Y. Pasholok, *Dolgozhdanniy istrebitel'*, https://warspot.ru/11413-dolgozhdannyy-istrebitel, retrieved on October 31st, 2023

WW2 Armor, *Every Tank a Tiger*, https://static1.squarespace.com/static/5d1810846e4b69000116772f/t/628bff3ddfe69644a55eb5dc/1653342015793/Every+Tank+a+Tiger.pdf, retrieved on December 14th, 2023

T. Schwallie, *Interview with Steven Zaloga*, https://tankandafvnews.com/2015/01/27/zaloga_interview/, retrieved on February 16th, 2024

Y. Pasholok, *IS s Tyazhelym Vooruzheniyev*, https://warspot.ru/11233-is-s-tyazhyolym-vooruzheniem, retrieved on November 1st, 2023

Y. Pasholok, *Kutsak Kotina*, https://warspot.ru/10800-kutsak-kotina, retrieved on October 31st, 2023

Y. Pasholok, *KV-3: Nabor tankovoy massy*, https://warspot.ru/4960-kv-3-nabor-tankovoy-massy, retrieved on November 3rd, 2023

P. Samsonov, *Landships Left in Port*, https://www.tankarchives.ca/2023/05/landships-left-in-port.html, retrieved on December 6th, 2023

International Molybdenum Association, *Molybdenum and its Applications - Iron, Steel, and Other Alloys*, https://www.imoa.info/molybdenum-uses/molybdenum-grade-stainless-steels/molybdenum-stainless-steels.php, retrieved on February 16th, 2024

Y. Pasholok, *Optimalnaya modernizatsiya*, https://warspot.ru/13911-optimalnaya-modernizatsiya, retrieved on November 1st, 2023

Y. Pasholok, *Poslednee prishestviye 76-mm dyrokola*, https://dzen.ru/media/yuripasholok/poslednee-prishestvie-76mm-dyrokola-615656c882810e092430e260, retrieved on October 29th, 2023

Y. Pasholok, *Promezhutochnoye zveno*, https://warspot.ru/14603-promezhutochnoe-zveno, retrieved on November 5th, 2023

Y. Pasholok, *Pushki pobolshe dlya T-34 ili kak pytatsya v zaitsa zapikhnut' utku*, https://dzen.ru/media/yuripasholok/pushki-pobolshe-dlia-t34-ili-kak-pytatsia-v-zaica-zapihnut-utku-5f914951c2b29d2294eca2b0, retrieved on October 29th, 2023

Y. Pasholok, *Put' ot srednego shturmovika k srednemu istrebitelyu*, https://warspot.ru/10662-put-ot-srednego-shturmovika-k-srednemu-istrebitelyu, retrieved on October 30th, 2023

P. Samsonov, *Robkiy vyzov*, https://warspot.ru/19685-robkiy-vyzov, retrieved on December 6th, 2023

Y. Pasholok, *SAU zadom napered*, https://warspot.ru/12075-sau-zadom-naperyod, retrieved on December 7th, 2023

Y. Pasholok, *Shag v nuzhnom napravlenii*, https://warspot.ru/14932-shag-v-nuzhnom-napravlenii, retrieved on November 5th, 2023

Y. Pasholok, *Sovetskiye Istrebiteli Tankov s Krugovym Obstrelom*, https://warspot.ru/4819-u-20-sovetskie-istrebiteli-tankov-s-krugovym-obstrelom, retrieved on October 30th, 2023

Y. Pasholok, *Strashnee koshki zverya net*, https://warspot.ru/11907-strashnee-koshki-zverya-net, retrieved on November 1st, 2023

Y. Pasholok, *Sredniy istrebitel' po-amerikanski*, https://warspot.ru/16063-sredniy-istrebitel-po-amerikanski, retrieved on December 7th, 2023

Park Patriot, *Sredniy Tank T-34-85*, https://parkpatriot.ru/o-parke/tekhnika-parka/sredniy-tank-t-34-85_Tex_centr, retrieved on October 31st, 2023

Y. Pasholok, *SU-76 amerikanskogo proizvodstva*, https://warspot.ru/8112-su-76-amerikanskogo-proizvodstva, retrieved on November 27th, 2023

Y. Pasholok, *Tankostroyeniye na grani zdravogo smysla*, https://warspot.ru/4995-tankostroenie-na-grani-zdravogo-smysla, retrieved on November 2nd, 2023

Y. Pasholok, *Teoriya bronetankovykh zabluzhdeniy: seredina Velikoy Otechestvennoy*, https://warspot.ru/16316-teoriya-bronetankovyh-zabluzhdeniy-seredina-velikoy-otechestvennoy, retrieved on October 29th, 2023

D. Oscroft, *The Myth of Tiger 131*, https://tankmuseum.org/article/the_myth_of_tiger_131, retrieved on November 6th, 2023

P. Samsonov, *Tiger or Elephant?*, https://www.tankarchives.ca/2019/10/tiger-or-elephant.html, retrieved on October 26th, 2023

Y. Pasholok, *Tigr Porsche: zhertva gryaznoy konkurentsii*, https://warspot.ru/10435-tigr-porshe-zhertva-gryaznoy-konkurentsii, retrieved on February 16th, 2024

N. Saichuk, *Tigry iz Lvova*, https://warspot.ru/21311-tigry-iz-lvova, retrieved on November 5th, 2023

A. Volgin, *Tolstaya shkura nemetskogo zverya*, https://warspot.ru/16322-tolstaya-shkura-nemetskogo-zverintsa, retrieved on November 4th, 2023

Military Channel, *Top Ten Tanks #3: Tiger*, https://www.youtube.com/watch?v=qoyW83fdJi4

Y. Pasholok, *Tupikovoye usileniye*, https://warspot.ru/15249-tupikovoe-usilenie, retrieved on November 5th, 2023

P. Samsonov, *Turn up the HEAT*, https://www.tankarchives.ca/2019/10/turn-up-heat.html, retrieved on November 4th, 2023

Y. Pasholok, *Tyazheliy istrebitel' tankov*, https://warspot.ru/14162-tyazhyolyy-istrebitel-tankov, retrieved on October 29th, 2023

Y. Pasholok, *Tyazheliy Trofey*, https://warspot.ru/9797-tyazhyolyy-trofey, retrieved on October 26th, 2023

Y. Pasholok, *Tyazheliye trofei iz mesta proryva blokady Leningrada*, https://dzen.ru/a/Y7mBJbPX2DsnnkXi, retrieved on October 26th, 2023

N. Moran, *US Army Anti-Armor Firing Tests of 1944*, https://worldoftanks.com/en/news/history/chieftains-hatch-us-guns-vs-german-armor-part-1, retrieved on December 15th, 2023

Y. Pasholok, *V poluschage ot Tigra*, https://warspot.ru/10152-v-polushage-ot-tigra, retrieved on February 16th, 2024